TALES FROM THE HINDU DRAMATISTS

MORE WILDSIDE CLASSICS

Please see www.wildsidepress.com for a complete list!

TALES FROM THE HINDU DRAMATISTS

R. N. DUTTA, B.A., B.L.

WILDSIDE PRESS

TALES FROM THE HINDU DRAMATISTS

This edition published in 2006 by Wildside Press, LLC.
www.wildsidepress.com

To
The Hon'ble Sir Justice

Ashutosh Mookerjee, Saraswati, Kt.

C.S.I., M.A., D.L., D.S.C., F.R.A.S., F.R.S.E.

Vice-Chancellor of the University of Calcutta.

THIS BOOK
IS
DEDICATED

as a sincere token of the esteem and admiration of the

AUTHOR

for his eminent services to the cause of the

ADVANCEMENT OF LEARNING.

CONTENTS

SAKUNTALA

or

THE LOST RING

In ancient days, there was a mighty king of the Lunar dynasty by name Dushyanta. He was the king of Hastinapur. He once goes out a-hunting and in the pursuit of a deer comes near the hermitage of the sage Kanwa, the chief of the hermits, where some anchorites request him not to kill the deer. The king feels thirsty and was seeking water when he saw certain maidens of the hermits watering the favourite plants. One of them, an exquisitely beautiful and bashful maiden, named Sakuntala, received him. She was the daughter of the celestial nymph Menaka by the celebrated sage Viswamitra and foster-child of the hermit Kanwa. She is smitten with love at the first sight of the king, standing confused at the change of her own feeling. The love at first sight which the king conceives for her is of too deep a nature to be momentary. Struck by her beauty he exclaims:—

"Her lip is ruddy as an opening bud; her graceful arms resemble tender shoots; attractive as the bloom upon the tree, the glow of youth is spread on all her limbs."

Seizing an opportunity of addressing her, he soon feels that it is impossible for him to return to his capital. His limbs move forward, while his heart flies back, like a silken standard borne against the breeze. He seeks for opportunities for seeing her. With the thought about her haunting him by day and night, he finds no rest, and no pleasure even in his favourite recreation—sporting. Mathavya, the jester, friend and companion of the king, however, breaks the dull monotony of his anxious time. The opportunity which the king seeks offers itself. The hermits send an embassy to the king asking him to come over to the hermitage to guard their sacrifices. As he was making preparations for departure to the hermitage, Karavaka, a messenger from the queen-mother, arrives asking his presence at the city of Hastinapur.

He is at first at a loss to extricate himself from this difficulty but a thought strikes him and he acts upon it. He sends the jester as his substitute to the city. He is now at leisure to seek out the love-sick Sakuntala who is drooping on account of her love for the king and is discovered lying on a bed of flowers in an arbour. He comes to the hermitage, overhears her conversation with her two friends, shows himself and offers to wed her. For a second time, the lovers thus meet. He enquires of her parentage to see if there is any obstacle to their being united in marriage; whereupon Sakuntala asks her companion Priyambada to satisfy the king with an account of her birth. The king hearing the story of her birth asks the companion to get the consent of Sakuntala to be married to him according to the form known as *gandharva*.

Sakuntala requests the king to wait till her foster-father Kanwa, who had gone out on a pilgrimage, would come back and give his consent. But the king, becoming importunate, she at last gives her consent. They are married according to the *gandharva* form, on the condition that the issue of the marriage should occupy the throne of Hastinapur. She accepts from her lord a marriage-ring as the token of recognition.

The king then goes away, after having promised to shortly send his ministers and army to escort her to his Capital. When Kanwa returns to the hermitage, he becomes aware of what has transpired during his absence by his spiritual powers, and congratulates Sakuntala on having chosen a husband worthy of her in every respect. Next day, when Sakuntala is deeply absorbed in thoughts about her absent lord, the celebrated choleric sage Durvasa comes and demands the rights of hospitality. But he is not greeted with due courtesy by Sakuntala owing to her pre-occupied state. Upon this, the ascetic pronounces a curse that he whose thought has led her to forget her duties towards guests, would disown her.

Sakuntala does not hear it, but Priyambada hears it and by entreaties appeases the wrath of the sage, who being conciliated ordains that the curse would cease at the sight of some ornament of recognition.

Sakuntala becomes quick with child and in the seventh month of her pregnancy is sent by her foster-father to Hastinapur, in the company of her sister Gautami, and his two disciples Sarngarva and Saradwata. Priyambada stays in the hermitage. Sakuntala takes leave of the sacred grove in which she has been brought up, of her flowers, her gazelles and her friends.

The aged hermit of the grove thus expresses his feelings at the approaching loss of Sakuntala:—

"My heart is touched with sadness at the thought, 'Sakuntala must go to-day'; my throat is choked with flow of tears repressed; my sight is dimmed with pensiveness but if the grief of an old forest hermit is so great, how keen must be the pang a father feels when freshly parted from a cherished child!"

Then he calls upon the trees to give her a kindly farewell. They answer with the Kokila's melodious cry.

Thereupon the following good wishes are uttered by voices in the air:—

"Thy journey be auspicious; may the breeze, gentle and soothing, fan the cheek; may lakes, all bright with lily cups, delight thine eyes; the sun-beam's heat be cooled by shady trees; the dust beneath thy feet be the pollen of lotuses."

On their way, Sakuntala and her companions bathe in the Prachi Saraswati, when, as Fate would have it, she carelessly drops the ring of recognition into the river, being unaware of the fact at the time. At last they arrive at Hastinapur, and send words to the king.

The king asks his family priest Somarata to enquire of them the cause of their coming. Whereupon the priest meets them at the gate, knows the objects of their coming and informs the king of it. The curse of Durvasa does its work. The king denies Sakuntala. At the intercession of the priest, she and her companions are brought before the king. The king publicly repudiates her. As a last resource, Sakuntala bethinks herself of the ring given her by her husband, but on discovering that it is lost, abandons hope. Sarnagarva sharply remonstrates against the conduct of the king and presses the claim of Sakuntala.

Gentle and meek as Sakuntala is, she undauntedly gives vent to her moral indignation against the king. The disciples go away saying that the king would have to repent of it.

Sakuntala falls senseless on the ground. After a while, she revives, the priest then comes forward and asks the king to allow her to stay in his palace till her delivery. The king consents, and when Sakuntala is following the priest, Menaka with her irradiant form appears and taking hold of her daughter vanishes and goes to a celestial asylum. Everyone present there is astonished and frightened.

After this incident, one day while the king is out on inspection, a certain fisherman, charged with the theft of the royal signet-ring which he professes to have found inside a fish, is dragged along by constables before the king who, however, causes the poor accused to be set free, rewarding him handsomely for his find.

Recollection of his former love now returns to him. His strong and passionate love for Sakuntala surges upon him with doubled and redoubled-force.

Indulging in sorrow at his repudiation of Sakuntala, the king passes three long years; at the end of which Matali, Indra's charioteer, appears to ask the king's aid in vanquishing the demons. He makes his aerial voyage in Indra's car. While he is coming back from the realm of Indra, he alights on the hermitage of Maricha.

Here he sees a young boy tormenting a lion-whelp. Taking his hand, without knowing him to be his own son, he exclaims:—"If now the touch of but a stranger's child thus sends a thrill of joy through all my limbs, what transports must be awakened in the soul of that blest father from whose loins he sprang!"

From the vaunting speeches of the boy, the king gathers that the boy is a scion of the race of Puru. His heart everflows with affection for him. A collection of circumstantial evidence points the boy to be his son. The amulet on the boy indicates his parentage.

But while he is in a doubtful mood as to the parentage of the refractory boy, he meets the sage Maricha from whom he learns everything. The name of the boy is Sarvadamana, afterwards known as Bharata, the most famous king of the Lunar race, whose authority is said to have extended over a great part of India, and from whom India is to this day called Bharata or Bharatavarsa (the country or domain of Bharata.)

Soon after, he finds and recognises Sakuntala, with whom he is at length happily re-united.

VIKRAMORVASI

or

URVASI WON BY VALOUR

or

THE HERO AND THE NYMPH

In the Himalaya mountains, the nymphs of heaven, on re-turning from an assembly of the gods, are mourning over the loss of Urvasi, a fellow-nymph, who has been carried off by a demon. King Pururavas enters on his chariot, and on hearing the cause of their grief, hastens to the rescue of the nymph. He soon returns, after having vanquished the robber, and restores Urvasi to her heavenly companions. While carrying the nymph back to her friends in his chariot, he is enraptured by her beauty, falls in love with her and she with her deliverer. Urvasi being summoned before the throne of Indra, the lovers are soon obliged to part. When they part, Urvasi wishes to turn round once more to see the king.

She pretends that a straggling vine has caught her garland, and while feigning to disengage herself, she calls one of her friends to help her.

The friend replies:—

"I fear, this is no easy task. You seem entangled too fast to be set free: but, come what may, defend upon my friendship." The eyes of the king then meet those of Urvasi. They now part.

The king is now at Prayag, the modern Allahabad, his resi-dence. He walks in the garden of his palace, accompanied by a Brahman who is his confidential companion, and knows his love for Urvasi. The companion is so afraid of betraying what must remain a secret to everybody at court, and in particular to the queen, that he hides himself in a retired temple. There a female servant of the queen discovers him, and 'as a secret can no more rest in his breast than morning dew upon the grass,' she soon finds out from him why the king is so changed, since his return from the battle with the demon, and carries the tale to the queen. In the meantime, the king is in despair, and pours out his grief. Urvasi also is sighing for him. She suddenly descends with her friend through the air to meet him.

Both are at first invisible to him, and listen to his confession of love.

Then Urvasi writes a verse on a birch-leaf, and lets it fall near the bower where her beloved reclines.

Next, her friend becomes visible, and at last, Urvasi herself is introduced to the king. After a few moments, however, both Urvasi and her friend are called back by a messenger of the gods, and the king is left alone with his jester. He looks for the leaf on which Urvasi had first disclosed her love, but it is lost, carried away by the wind. But worse than this the leaf is picked up by the queen, who comes to look for the king in the garden. The queen severely upbraids her husband, and, after a while, goes off in a hurry, like a river in the rainy season.

When Urvasi was recalled to Indra's heaven, she had to act before Indra the part of the goddess of beauty, who selects Vishnu for her husband. One of the names of Vishnu is Purushottama.

Poor Urvasi, when called upon to confess on whom her heart was set, forgetting the part she had to act, says "I love Pururavas," instead of "I love Purushottama."

Her teacher Bharata, the author of the play, is so much exasperated by this mistake, that he pronounces a curse upon Urvasi. "You must lose your divine knowledge." After the close of the performance, Indra, observing her as she stood apart, ashamed and disconsolate, calls her and says:—

"The mortal, who engrosses your thoughts, has been my friend in the days of adversity; he has helped me in the conflict with the enemies of the gods, and is entitled to my acknowledgements. You must, accordingly, repair to him and remain with him till he beholds the offspring you shall bear him." The god thus permits her to marry the mortal hero.

After transacting public business, the king retires to the garden of the palace as the evening approaches. A messenger arrives from the queen, apprising his Majesty that she desires to see him on the terrace of the pavilion. The king obeys and ascends the crystal steps while the moon is just about to rise, and the east is tinged with red.

As he is waiting for the queen, his desire for Urvasi is awakened again. On a sudden, Urvasi enters on a heavenly car, accompanied by his friend. They are invisible to the king as on the previous occasion. The moment that Urvasi is about to withdraw her veil, the queen appears. She is dressed in white, without any ornaments, and comes to propitiate her husband, by taking a vow.

Then she, calling upon the god of the moon, performs her solemn vow and retires.

Urvasi, who is present, though in an invisible state, during this scene of matrimonial reconciliation, now advances behind the king and covers his eyes with her hands. The king says:—

"It must be Urvasi; no other hand could shed such ecstasy through my emaciated frame. The solar rays do not wake the night's fair blossom; that alone expands when conscious of the moon's dear presence."

She takes the resignation of the queen in good earnest and claims the king as granted her by right. Her friend takes leave and she now remains with the king as his beloved wife in the groves of a forest.

Subsequently the lovers are wandering near Kailasa, the divine mountain, when Urvasi, in a fit of jealousy, enters the grove of Kumara, the god of war, which is forbidden to all females. In consequence of Bharat's curse she is instantly metamorphosed into a creeper. The king beside himself with grief at her loss, seeks her everywhere. The nymphs in a chorus deplore her fate. Mournful strains are heard in the air.

The king enters a wild forest, his features express insanity, his dress is disordered. Clouds gather overhead. He rushes frantically after a cloud which he mistakes for a demon that carried away his bride.

He addresses various birds and asks them whether they have seen his love,—the peacock, 'the bird of the dark-blue throat and eyes of jet,'—the cuckoo, 'whom lovers deem Love's messenger,'— the swans, 'who are sailing northward, and whose elegant gait betrays that they have seen her,'—the chakravaka, 'a bird who, during the night, is himself separated from his mate,'—but none responds. He apostrophises various insects, beasts and even a mountain peak to tell him where she is.

Neither the bees which murmur amidst the petals of the lotus, nor the royal elephant, that reclines with his mate under the Kadamba tree, has seen the lost one.

At last he thinks he sees her in the mountain stream:—

"The rippling wave is like her frown; the row of tossing birds her girdle; streaks of foam, her fluttering garment as she speeds along; the current, her devious and stumbling gait. It is she turned in her wrath into a stream."

At last the king finds a gem of ruddy radiance. He holds it in his hands, and embraces the vine which is now transformed into Urvasi. Thus is she restored to her proper form, through the mighty spell of the magical gem. The efficacious gem is placed on her forehead. The king recovers his reason. They are thus happily re-united and return to Allahabad.

Several years elapse. An unlucky incident now comes to pass. A hawk bears away the ruby of re-union. Orders are sent to shoot the bird, and, after a short while, a forester brings the jewel and the arrow by which the hawk was killed. An inscription on the shaft shows that its owner is Ayus. A female ascetic enters, leading a boy with a bow in hand.

The boy is Ayus, the son of Urvasi, whom his mother confided to the female ascetic who generously brought him up in the forest and now; sends him back to his mother. The king who was not aware that Urvasi had ever borne him a son, now recognises Ayus as his son. Urvasi also comes to embrace her boy. She now suddenly bursts into tears and tells the king:—

"Indra decreed that I am to be recalled to heaven when you see our son. This induced me to conceal from you so long the birth of the child. Now that you have accidentally seen the child, I shall have to return to heaven, in compliance with the decree of Indra."

She now prepares to leave her husband after she has seen her boy installed as associate king. So preparations are made for the inauguration ceremony when Narada the messenger of Indra, comes to announce that the god has compassionately revoked the decree. The nymph is thus permitted to remain on earth for good as the hero's second wife.

Nymphs descend from heaven with a golden vase containing the water of the heavenly Ganges, a throne, and other paraphernalia, which they arrange. The prince is inaugurated as Yuvaraj. All now go together to pay their homage to the queen, who had so generously resigned her rights in favour of Urvasi.

MALAVIKAGNIMITRA

or

AGNIMITRA AND MALAVIKA

We learn a wise sentiment from the prologue. The stage-manager, addressing the audience, says:—"All that is old is not, on that account, worthy of praise, nor is a novelty, by reason of its newness, to be censured. The wise do not decide what is good or bad till they have tested merit for themselves: a foolish man trusts to another's judgement."

Puspamitra was the founder of the Sunga dynasty of Magadha kings, having been the general of Vrihadratha, the last of the Maurya race, whom he deposed and put to death: he was succeeded by his son Agnimitra who reigned at Vidica (Bhilsa) in the second century B.C. King Agnimitra has two queens Dharini and Iravati. Malavika belongs to the train of his queen Dharini's attendants. The maid was sent as a present to the queen by her brother, Virsena, governor of the Antapala or barrier-fortress on the Nermada.

The queen jealously keeps her out of the king's sight on account of her great beauty. The king, however, accidentally sees the picture of Malavika, painted by order of the queen for her *chitrasala*, or picture-gallery. The sight of the picture inspires the king with an ardent desire to view the original, whom he has never yet beheld.

Hostilities are about to break out between Agnimitra and Yajnasena, king of Viderbha (Berar). The first, on one occasion, had detained captive the brother-in-law of the latter, and Yajnasena had retaliated by throwing into captivity Madhavasena, the personal friend of Agnimitra, when about to repair to Vidisa to visit that monarch. Yajnasena sends to propose an exchange of prisoners, but Agnimitra haughtily rejects the stipulation, and sends orders to his brother-in-law, Virasena, to lead an army immediately against the Raja of Viderbha. This affair being disposed of, he directs his attention to domestic interests, and employs his Vidushaka or confidant, Gotama, to procure him the sight of Malavika. To effect this, Gotama instigates a quarrel between the professors, Ganadas and Haradatta, regarding their respective pre-eminence.

They appeal to the Raja, who, in consideration of Ganadasa's being patronised by the queen, refers the dispute to her. She is induced to consent reluctantly to preside at a trial of skill between the parties, as shown in the respective proficiency of their select scholars. The queen is assisted by a protegé, a *Parivrajaka*, or female ascetic and woman of superior learning.

The party assembles in the chamber where the performance is to take place, fitted up with the *Sangitarachana*, or orchestral decorations. The king's object is attained, for Ganadasa brings forward Malavika as the pupil on whom he stakes his credit. Malavika sings an *Upanga* or prelude, and then executes an air of extraordinary difficulty. Malavika's performance is highly applauded, and, of course, captivates the king and destroys his peace of mind; the Vidushaka detains her until the queen, who has all along suspected the plot, commands her to retire. The warder cries the hour of noon, on which the party breaks up, and the queen, with more housewifery than majesty, hastens away to expedite her royal husband's dinner.

There stands an *asoka* tree in the garden. The Hindus believe that this tree, when barren, may be induced to put forth flowers by the contact of the foot of a handsome woman. The tree in question does not blossom, and being the favourite of Dharini, she has proposed to try the effect of her own foot. Unluckily however, the Vidhushaka, whilst setting her swing in motion, has tumbled her out of it and the fall has sprained her ankle, so that she cannot perform the ceremony herself: she therefore deputes Malavika to do it for her, who accordingly comes to the spot attired in royal habiliments, and accompanied by her friend Vakulavali. In the conversation that ensues, she acknowledges her passion for the king, who with his friend Gotama has been watching behind the tree, and overhears the declaration; he therefore makes his appearance and addresses a civil speech, to Malavika when he is interrupted by another pair of listeners, Iravati and her attendant. She commands Malavika's retreat, and leaves the king, in a violent rage, to inform Dharini of what is going forward. The King never behaves as a despot but always with much consideration for the feelings of his spouses.

The Vidushika now informs the king that Malavika has been locked in the *Sarabhandagriha* or the store or treasure room by the queen. The room was no enviable place, as the Vidusaka compares it to Patala, the infernal regions. He undertakes, however, to effect her liberation; and whilst he prepares for his scheme, the Raja pays a visit to the queen.

Whilst the Raja is engaged in tranquil conversation with

Dharini, and the parivrajaka, the vidushaka rushes in, exclaiming he has been beaten by a venomous snake, whilst gathering flowers to bring with him as a present on his visit to the queen, and he exhibits his thumb bound with his cord, and marked with the impressions made by the teeth of the reptile. The parivrajaka, with some humour as well as good surgery, recommends the actual cautery, or the amputation of the thumb; but the vidushaka pretending to be in convulsions and dying, the snake-doctor is sent for, who having had his clue refuses to come, and desires the patient may be sent to him: the vidushaka is accordingly sent. The queen is in great alarm, as being, however innocently, the cause of a Brahman's death. Presently the messenger returns, stating that the only hope is the application of the snake-stone to the bite, and requesting the Raja to order one to be procured: the queen has one in her finger-ring, which she instantly takes off and sends to the vidushaka. This is his object, for the female jailor of Malavika has, as he has ascertained, been instructed to liberate her prisoner only on being shown the seal ring or signet of the queen, and having got this in his possession, he immediately effects the damsel's release, after which the ring is returned to the queen, and the Vidushaka is perfectly recovered.

The king then being summoned away by a concerted pretext, hastens to the Samudra pavilion, where Malavika has been conveyed with her friend and companion, Vakulavali. This pavilion is decorated with portraits of the king and his queens, and Malavika is found by her lover engrossed with their contemplation. Vakulavali retires. The Vidushaka takes charge of the door, but he no sooner sits down on the threshold than he falls asleep. The Raja and Malavika, consequently, have scarcely time to exchange professions of regard, when they are again disturbed by the vigilant and jealous Iravati, who sends information of her discoveries to Dharini, and in the meantime remains sentinel over the culprits. The party, however, is disturbed by news, that Agnimitra's daughter has been almost frightened to death by a monkey, and Iravati and the Raja hasten to her assistance, leaving Malavika to the consolation derived from hearing that the *Asoka* tree is in blossom, an omen of the final success of her own desires.

The Raja, Dharini and the Parivrajaka, with Malavika and other attendants, gather about the *Asoka* tree, when some presents arrive from the now submissive monarch of Viderbha, against whom the troops of Virashena have been successful. Amongst the gifts are two female slaves, who immediately recognize in Malavika the sister of Madhavasena, the friend of Agnimitra, whom the armies of the latter have just extricated from the captivity to which the Viderbha sovereign had consigned him. It appears that when he was formerly seized by his kinsman, his minister, Sumati, contrived to effect his own escape, along with his sister and the young princess. That sister, Kausika, now reveals herself in the person of the Parivrajaka, and continues the story of their flight. Sumati joined a caravan bound to Vidisa On their way to the Vindhya mountains, they were attacked by the foresters, who were armed with bows and arrows, and decorated with peacock's plumes: in the affray Sumati was slain and Malavika was lost.

Kausika, left alone, committed her brother's body to the flames, and then resumed her route to Vidisa, where she assumed the character of a female ascetic The Raja observes she did wisely. Kausika soon found out Malavika, but forebore to discover herself, confiding in the prophecy of a sage, who had foretold that the princess, after passing through a period of servitude, would meet with a suitable match.

It thus finally turns out that Malavika is by birth a princess, who had only come to be an attendant at Agnimitra's court through having fallen into the hands of robbers.

The king issues his orders respecting the terms to be granted to Yajnasena, the king of Viderbha, the half of whose territory he assigns to Madhavasena, the brother of Malavika.

A letter arrives from the general Pushpamitra, giving an account of some transactions that have occurred upon the southern bank of the Indus.

On his own behalf, or that of his son, he had undertaken to celebrate an *aswamedha*, or horse-sacrifice, for which it was essential that the steed should have a free range for twelve months, being attended only by a guard to secure him. This guard had been placed by Pushpamitra under the command of Agnimitra's son, Vasumitra. Whilst following the victim along the Indus, a party of Yavana horse attempted to carry off the courser, but they were encountered by the young prince, and after a sharp conflict, defeated.

Pushpamitra concludes with inviting his son to come with his family to complete the sacrifice.

The queen, Dharini, overjoyed with the news of her son's success and safety, distributes rich presents to all her train and the females of Agnimitra's establishment, whilst to him she presents Malavika. Iravati communicates her concurrence in this arrangement, and the Raja obtains a bride, whom his queens accept as their sister. The difficulty of conciliating his queens is thus removed. The king now marries Malavika and all ends happily.

THE VIRA CHARITA OR
THE MAHAVIRA CHARITA

or

THE LIFE OF THE GREAT HERO

Dasaratha, the king of Ayodhya (Oudh), is the father of four sons Rama, Lakshmana, Bharata and Satrughna. Rama and Lakshmana visit Viswamitra's hermitage. Kusadhwaja, the king of Sankasya and the brother of Janaka, the king of Mithila, accompanied by his two nieces, Sita and Urmila, enters the hermitage of Viswamitra on the borders of the Kausiki (Cosi), having been invited by the sage to his sacrifice. He is met by the sage with the two youths Rama and Lakshmana, and the young couples become mutually enamoured. Meanwhile Ahalya—the cursed wife of Gautama—gets cleared of her guilt through the purifying influence of Rama.

A messenger from Ravana, the demon king of Lanka, arrives, who has followed them from Mithila, and comes to demand Sita as a wife for his master.

They are further disturbed by Taraka, a female fiend, the daughter of Suketu, wife of Sunda and mother of Maricha. Rama, by command of Viswamitra slays her. Viswamitra is exceedingly pleased with the deed and invokes and gives to Rama the heavenly weapons with all their secrets of discharge and dissolution. The sage recommends Kusadhwaja to invite the bow of Siva for Rama's present trial, and consequent obtaining of Sita. The bow arrives, self-conveyed, being, as the weapon of so great a deity, pregnant with intelligence. Rama snaps it asunder, in consequence of which feat it is agreed that Sita shall be wedded to him; Urmila her sister, to Lakshmana; and Mandavi and Srutakirti, the daughters of Kusadhwaja, to Bharata and Satrughna respectively. The party is again disturbed by Suvahu and Maricha, the first of whom is killed and the second, thrown at a distance by Rama.

The messenger of Ravana then goes away mortified to represent the matter to the minister of Ravana. The saint and his visitors then retire into the hermitage.

Malyavan, the minister and maternal grandfather of Ravana and the king's sister Surpanakha have heard the news of Rama's wedding with Sita from Siddhasrama and discuss the consequences with some apprehension. The minister takes the marriage as an insult to his master.

A letter arrives from Parasurama partly requesting and partly commanding Ravana to call off some of his imps, who are molesting the sages in Dandakaranya. He writes from Mahendra Dwipa.

Malyavan takes advantage of this opportunity to instigate a quarrel between the two Ramas, anticipating that Parasurama, who is the pupil of Siva, will be highly incensed when he hears of Rama's breaking the bow of that divinity. The hero comes to Videha, the palace of Janaka, to defy the insulter of his god and preceptor. He enters the interior of the palace, the guards and attendants being afraid to stop him, and calls upon Rama to show himself. The young hero is proud of Parasurama's seeking him and anxious for the encounter but detained awhile by Sita's terrors: at last the heroes meet. Parasurama alludes to his own history how he, having overcome his fellow-pupil, Kartikeya, in a battle-axe fight, received his axe from his preceptor, Siva, as the prize of his prowess.

Parasurama addresses Rama thus:—

"How dost thou presume to bend thy brow in frowns on me? Thou must be an audacious boy, a scion of the vile Kshatriya race. Thy tender years and newly wedded bride teach me a weakness I am not wont to feel.

"Throughout the world the story runs, I, Rama, and the son of Jamadgni, struck off a mother's head with remorseless arm. This vengeful axe has one and twenty times destroyed the Kshatriya race, not sparing in its wrath the unborn babe hewn piecemeal in the parent womb.

"It was thus I slaked the fires of a wronged father's wrath with blood, whose torrents, drawn unsparingly from martial veins, fed the vast reservoir in which I love to bathe."

Rama replies thus:—

"Give over thy vaunts—I hold thy cruelty a crime, not virtue."

The combat between the two Ramas is suspended by the arrival of Janaka and Satananda, and Rama's being summoned to attend the Kanchana Mochana, the loosening of Sita's golden bracelet.

Parasurama awaits Ramachandra's return. He is accosted in succession by Vasishtha, Viswamitra, Satananda, Janaka and Dasaratha, who first endeavour to soothe and then to terrify him; but he outbullies them all: at last Ramachandra returns from the string-removing ceremony and is heard calling on Parasurama, and the combat ensues. Ramachandra comes out victorious.

The two kings Janaka and Dasaratha congratulate each other

on the victory of Ramachandra. Parasurama is now as humble as he was before arrogant: he calls upon the earth to hide his shame. Whilst Rama regrets Bhargava's departure, Surpanakha, disguised as Manthara, the favourite of Kaikeyi, Dasaratha's second wife, arrives with a letter to Rama, requesting him to use his influence with his father to secure Kaikeyi the two boons which Dasaratha was pledged to grant her; specifying one to be her son Bharata's inauguration, and the other, assent to Rama's voluntary exile. In the meantime, Dasaratha, who has determined to raise Rama to the participation of regal dignity, communicates his intention to his son. Rama replies by informing him of Kaikeyi's message, and is earnest with his father to accede to her request.

Bharata and his maternal uncle Yuddhajit arrive, and ask Dasaratha to crown Rama and all are full of wonder and concern: however, as there is no help for it, Dasaratha consents and orders preparations for the ceremony.

Lakshmana and Sita are alone to accompany Rama, on which her father Janaka exclaims, "My child, what happiness it will be to wait upon thy husband in the hour of trouble, permitted to partake and cheer his wanderings!" Bharata requests permission to go with them, but Rama refuses his assent; on which his brother begs his golden shoes of him, promising to instal them in the kingdom, and rule thereafter as their representative. The seniors are led out in deep despondency, and Rama with his brother and wife set off to the woods.

A dialogue opens between the two birds, Jatayu and Sampati, the vulture-descendants of Kasyapa, who have seen successive creations. They relate Rama's progress towards the south; and Sampati, the elder leaves his brother Jatayu, with strict injunctions to assist Rama, if needed. He then goes to the ocean to perform daily duties and Jatayu to Malaya. Jatayu perches on the mountain and marks the hero Rama in pursuit of the swift deer. Lakshmana directs his remote course thither. A holy seer approaches the bower and the dame gives him meet welcome. His form expands.

It is he, the felon Ravana—his train crowd from the groves; he seizes upon Sita—he mounts the car. Jatayu cries shame on his birth and threatens to rend his limbs and revel in his gore. Jatayu is, however, killed in the conflict. Rama raves with indignation. The brothers set off in pursuit of the ravisher, when Sramana, a female devotee sent by Vibhishana to Rama, calls for succour being seized by Kabandha, a headless fiend. Rama sends Lakshmana to her rescue; he goes off to kill the demon and returns with the dame. She gives Rama a note from Vibhishana praying for his refuge. Rama asks Lakshmana what reply to be sent to (his) "dear friend—lord of Lanka" and Lakshman replies that those words are sufficient.

(Two promises are implied—first contraction of friendship and secondly bestowal of the Kingdom of Lanka.)

Rama, learning from the devotee that Vibhishana is with Sugriva, Hanuman, and other monkey chiefs at Rishyamuka, and that the monkeys have picked up Sita's ornaments and upper garments in the forest, determines to go to them. Kabandha then appears, to thank Rama for killing him, being thereby liberated from a curse and restored to a divine condition.

They then set off to Rishyamuka, the residence of Bali, watered by the Pampa. In the way Rama performs a miracle by kicking away the skeleton of a giant.

When the brothers arrive at the mountain, Bali appears like a cloud upon its peak and, being instigated by his friend Malyavan, resolves to oppose Rama. The heroes meet and, after exchange of civilities, go to the conflict.

The noise brings Vibhishana, Sugriva, and all the monkey chiefs to the place. Bali is overthrown and mortally wounded. He recommends the Monkeys to choose Sugriva and his own son Angada for their joint sovereigns, and mediates an alliance between Rama and them, as well as with Vibhishana. Rama and Sugriva pledge themselves to eternal friendship, over the sacrificial fire in Matanga's hermitage which stood close by. Bali then repeats his request to the monkey chiefs, as they were attached to him, to acknowledge Sugriva and Angada as their joint leaders, and to follow them in aid of Rama against Ravana in the ensuing contest: he then dies.

Malyavan laments over these miscarriages. Trijata, a Rakshasi, adds to his despondency by news of the mischief inflicted by Hanumana, who has burnt the town of Lanka and slain a son of Ravana. He goes off to set guards, and gather news by means of spies.

Ravana meditates on his love. His queen Mahodhari comes to bring him tidings of Rama's approach, but he only laughs at her. She tells him of the bridge made by Rama: he replies, if all the mountains of the earth were cast into the ocean, they would not furnish footing to cross it. His incredulity is terminated by a general alarm, and the appearance of Prahasta, his general, to announce that Lanka is invested. Angada comes as envoy from Rama, to command Ravana to restore Sita and prostrate himself and his family at the feet of Lakshmana. Ravana, enraged, orders some contumely or punishment to be inflicted upon him. He orders him to be shaved. Angada puffs his hair out with rage. The monkey tells Ravana, if he were not an ambassador, he would tear off his ten heads, and he then springs away; the tumult increases, and Ravana goes forth to the combat. Indra and Chiraratha then come to see the battle from the air.

All the chiefs of the two parties engage in promiscuous war. The Rakshasas have the worst, but Ravana, with his brother Kumbhakarna and his son Meghanada, turns the tide: the monkeys fly, leaving Rama almost unsupported. Lakshmana attacks Meghanada: Ravana quits Rama to assist his son.

The "serpent band" of Meghnada is dispersed by the "eagle-king-weapon" of Lakshmana. The forces of Kumbhakarna are reduced to ashes with a fire-weapon by Rama. Rama kills Kumbhakarna, and then goes to the aid of Lakshmana; the whole of Rama's party are then overwhelmed with magical weapons, hurled invisibly by Ravana upon them, and fall senseless. While Ravana seeks to restore Kumbhakarna, Hanuman, reviving, goes to fetch *amrita*, and tearing up the mountain that contains it, returns to the field: his very approach restores Lakshmana, who jumps up with increased animation, like a serpent starting from his shrivelled skin or the sun bursting from clouds. So Raghu's youngest hope, restored by heavenly herbs, burns with more than wonted ardour, wonders a moment what has chanced and then, all on fire for glory, rushes to the fight. Rama also revives, and instigated by the sages, exerts his celestial energies, by which the daitya, Ravana, and his host speedily perish. Rama is victorious, and Sita is recovered.

Vibhishana is now crowned king of Lanka. Alaka, a tutelary deity, comes. Lanka, another tutelary deity, is consoled by Alaka.

Sita passes the fiery ordeal in triumph. The gods cheer her.

Rama, accompainied by Sita, Lakshmana, Vibhishana and Sugriva, then enters the aerial car Pushpaka which was once wrested from Kuvera by Ravana, and which is now placed at the disposal of Rama by Vibhishana. The car transports them from Ceylon all the way to Ayodhya. One or other of the party points out the places over which they fly viz. the *Setu* or bridge of Rama the Malaya mountain, the Kaveri river, the hermitage of Agastya, the Pampa river, the residence of Bali and of Jatayu, the limits of the Dandaka forest, the Sahya or Sailadri mountains and the boundaries of Aryavarta.

They then rise and travel through the upper air, approaching near the sun, and are met and eulogized by a *Kinnara* and his bride; they then come to the peaks of the Himalaya, and descend upon Tapavana, whence they go towards Ayodhya, where Rama is welcomed by his brothers Bharata and Satrughna, their mothers, Vasistha and Viswamitra.

The four brothers embrace one another. Rama is now consecrated king by Vasishtha and Viswamitra.

UTTAR RAMA CHARITA

or

THE LATER LIFE OF RAMA

Rama, when duly crowned at Ayodhya, enters upon a life of quiet enjoyment with his wife Sita. The love of Rama and Sita, purified by sorrow during the late exile, is most tender.

After a stay of a few days at Ayodhya, Janaka, the father of Sita, goes back to his country Mithila. Rama consoles his queen for her father's absence. The sage Ashtavakra comes in and delivers a message to Rama from his spiritual preceptors to satisfy the wishes of Sita and please his people. Then the sage goes away.

The family priest Vasishtha, having to leave the capital for a time to assist at a sacrifice, utters a few words of parting advice to Rama, thus:—

"Remember that a king's real glory consists in his people's welfare."

Rama replies: "I am ready to give up everything, happiness, love, pity—even Sita herself—if needful for my subjects' good."

In accordance with this promise, he employs an emissary named Durmukha to ascertain the popular opinion as to his own treatment of his subjects.

Lakshmana now asks Rama and Sita to come out and see their early history drawn on the terrace of the palace. They move about and the different parts of the picture are shown to Sita, when the eyes of Sita turn on the 'yawn-producing' weapons. Rama asks her to salute them so that they would attend also on her children. Sita then feels tired and lays her head on the arm of her husband and sleeps.

Then Durmukha, who, as an old and trusted servant, had free admission to the inner apartments, comes and whispers to him that people condemn his receiving back a queen, abducted by a fiend, after her long residence in a stranger's house. In short, he is told that they still gossip and talk scandal about her and Ravana. The scrupulously correct and over-sensitive Rama, though convinced of his wife's fidelity after her submission to the fiery ordeal, and though she is now likely to become a mother, feels himself quite unable to allow the slightest cause of offence to continue among his subjects.

He has no other resource. People must be satisfied. He orders his dear Sita's exile, and the messenger goes away to deliver the order to Lakshmana to seclude her somewhere in the woods. He is torn by contending feelings. He is overpowered with grief, withdraws his arm from his sleeping wife and pours forth pathetic lamentation. Then he takes up her feet and cries when the announcement of the arrival of frightened Rishis makes him go out to send Satrughna to their succour. The messenger Durmukha then enters and takes Sita unsuspectingly to mount the chariot which is to lead her to exile.

Lakshmana takes Sita to the forest and leaves her there.

She is protected by divine agencies. Her twin sons, Kusa and Lava, are born and entrusted to the care of the sage Valmiki, the author of the Ramayana, who brings them up in his hermitage. The boys have no knowledge of their royal descent.

An incident now occurs which leads Rama to revisit the Dandaka forest, the scene of his former exile. The child of a Brahman dies suddenly and unaccountably. His body is laid at Rama's door. Evidently some national sin is the cause of such a calamity, and an aerial voice informs him that an awful crime is being perpetrated; for a Sudra, named Sambuka, is practising religious austerities, instead of confining himself to his proper vocation of waiting on the twice-born castes. Rama instantly starts for the forest, discovers Sambuka in the sacrilegious act and strikes off his head. But death by Rama's hand confers immortality on the Sudra, who appears as a celestial spirit, and thanks his benefactor for the glory and felicity thus obtained.

Before returning to Ayodhya, Rama is induced to visit the hermitage of the sage Agastya in Panchavati. Sita now reappears. She is herself invisible to Rama through the favour of the Bhagirathi but able to thrill with emotions by her touch. Rama is greatly distracted.

He faints with old remembrances but revives on the touch of Sita. He observes, "What does this mean? Heavenly balm seems poured into my heart; a well-known touch changes my insensibility to life. Is it Sita, or am I dreaming?"

He vainly seeks for her possession, but at last goes away on the advice of his companion Visanti.

The sage Valmiki makes great preparations for receiving Vasishtha, Janaka, Kaushalya, the mother of Rama and other eminent guests. The pupils are delighted because the visit of the guests affords hopes of a feast at which flesh meat is to constitute one of the dishes.

As the boys have got a holiday in honour of the guests, they are playing at some distance from a tree outside the hermitage. Among them, Kaushalya notices a boy with the features of her son, who is called in but whom the guests do not yet know to be a son of Rama.

Soon after, the horse of the horse-sacrifice of Rama comes near and he goes out with other boys to see the fun while the elders go to see the host.

The attendant soldiers cry out that Rama is the only hero of the world. Lava—for such is the boy's name,—cannot brook such vaunts and removes the banner. Soldiers crowd upon him and Lava draws his bow. Lakshmana's son Chandraketu—the general of the army—arrives surprised at the slaughter of his army and asks Lava to leave the incapable army and fight with himself. Lava obeys the call and after some conversation in which he ridicules the powers of Rama and infuriates his antagonist, they go out to fight.

The discharge and repulsion of the divine weapons occur.

The approach of Rama puts an end to the contest. Lava's elder brother Kusa has heard of his fight and comes to "eradicate from the world the name of emperor." But Lava has become calm and asks his brother to pay respects to the hero of the Ramayana.

Rama embraces both of them and is moved with their son-like touch. He notices in them the features of his wife He knows that his children alone could possess the divine weapons. He recollects that his wife was left in that part of the forest and instinctively comes to the conclusion that they are his children. He wishes to ask about their birth in a roundabout way, but before proceeding to the end, is asked to see his spiritual preceptor.

The desertion of Sita is acted by nymphs on the banks of the Ganges before Rama and other high guests invited by Valmiki.

Sita, from behind the stage, cries out "the beasts of prey desire [to devour] me in the forest (left) alone and unprotected. I will throw myself into the Bhagirathi." She enters supported by her mother Prithivi, the Earth and Ganga, each carrying a baby in the lap. Ganga tells her of the birth of the twins and consoles her, but Earth is greatly distressed with the conduct of Rama. Ganga replies "who can close the door of Fate?"

But Earth says, "has it been proper for the good Rama? He disregarded the hand he pressed when a boy. He disregarded me and Janaka. He disregarded Fire (who shewed her purity). He disregarded the children she was about to bring forth."

But Ganga pacifies her and they agree to make over the children to Valmiki, when they become a little old. Earth then asks her daughter to come to the nether world, to which she agrees and with their exit closes the play.

At the close of the play, Rama faints. Then the real Sita enters with Arundhuti, the wife of Rama's preceptor and touches and revives her husband. The people are satisfied with her purity and Rama takes her back with the children who are introduced by Valmiki. The husband and wife are thus re-united after twelve years of grievous solitude, and happiness is restored to the whole family. The re-union is witnessed not only by the people of Ayodhya, but by the congregated deities of earth and heaven.

Rama thus describes his love for his wife:—

"Her presence is ambrosia to my sight; her contact, fragrant sandal; her fond arms, twined round my neck; are a far richer clasp than costliest gems, and in my house she reigns the guardian goddess of my fame and fortune. Oh! I could never bear again to lose her."

MALATI AND MADHAVA

or

THE STOLEN MARRIAGE

There lived, in the town of Kundinapura in Berar, Devarata, a very calm and sagacious minister to the king of Vidarbha. He had a son named Madhava. Madhava was very beautiful and of uncommon intelligence. He became proficient in all branches of learning, in his early age. He now arrived at a marriageable age. The beautiful town of Padmavati in Malwa is situated at the confluence of the two rivers Indus and Madhumati. There lived in Padmavati, Bhurivasu, who was minister to the king of Padmavati. He had a very beautiful unmarried daughter named Malati. The king indicated an intention to propose a match between Malati and his own favourite Nandan, who was both old and ugly, and whom she detested. Bhurivasu feared to give offence to the king by refusing the match. Devarata and Bhurivasu were fellow students. In their academical days they pledged themselves that they should enter into matrimonial alliance, if they happen to have children. Malati and Madhava did not know anything about their fathers' promises. There lived in Padmavati, Kamandaki, an old Buddhist priestess who was nurse of Malati. The priestess knew everything about the matrimonial promise. She was a very intelligent lady and was respected by all. The two friends concert a plan with the priestess to throw the young people in each other's way and to connive at a secret marriage. In pursuance of this scheme, Madhava is sent to finish his studies at the city of Padmavati with the ostensible object of studying Logic under the care of the priestess, who takes great care of her pupil and endeavours her utmost to fulfil the promise of her two friends. By her contrivance and with the aid of Malati's foster-sister Lavangika, the young people meet and become mutually enamoured.

Kamandaki addresses her favourite disciple Avalokita thus:—

"Dear Avalokita! Oh how I wish for the marital union of Madhava, the son of Devarata, and Malati, the daughter of Bhurivasu! Auspicious signs forerun a happy fate. Even now my throbbing eyeball tells that propitious destiny shall crown my schemes."

Avalokita replies:—

"Oh, here is a serious cause of anxiety. How strange! You are already burdened with the austerities of devotional exercises, Bhurivasu has commissioned you to perform this arduous task.

Though retired from the world, you could not avoid this business."

Kamandaki says, "Never say so. The commission is an office of love and trust. If my friend's object is gained even at the expense of my life and penances, I shall feel myself gratified."

The pupil asks "why is a stolen marriage intended?"

The priestess answers, "Nandana, a favourite of the king of Padmavati, sues him for Malati. The king demands the maiden of her father. To evade the anger of the king, this ingenious device has been adopted. Let the world deem their union was the work of mutual passion only. So the king and Nandan will be foiled. A wise man veils his projects from the world." The pupil says, "I take Madhava to walk in the street in front of the house of the minister Bhurivasu."

The priestess says,

"I have heard from Lavangika, the foster-sister of Malati, that Malati has seen Madhava from the windows of her house. Her waning form faithfully betrays the lurking care she now first learns to suffer."

The pupil says, "I have heard that, to soothe that care, Malati has drawn a picture of Madhava and has sent it through Lavangika to Mandarika, her attendant."

The priestess perceives that Malati has done so with the object that the picture would reach Madhava as Mandarika is in love with Kalahansa, the servant of Madhava. Avalokita again says,

"To-day is the great festival of Madan; Malati will surely come to join the festival, I have interested Madhava to go to the garden of Love's god with a view that the youthful pair may meet there."

The priestess replies, "I tender my best thanks for your kindly zeal to aid the object of my wishes. Can you give me any tidings of Soudamini, my former pupil?"

Avalokita answers, "she now resides upon mount *Sriparvata*. She has now arrived at supernatural power by religious austerities. I have learnt the news about her from Kapala Kundala, the female pupil of a tremendous magician Aghorghanta, a seer and a wandering mendicant, but now residing amidst the neighbouring forest, who frequents the temple of the dreadful goddess *Chamunda* near the city cemetry." Avalokita remarks, "Madhava would be highly pleased if his early friend Makaranda is united in wedlock with Madayantika, the sister of Nandana."

The priestess observes, "I have already engaged my disciple Buddharakshita for the purpose. Let us go forth and having learnt how Madhava has fared, repair to Malati. May our devices prosper!"

Madhava thus describes to his friend Makaranda his first interview with Malati, and acknowledges himself deeply smitten:—

"One day, advised by Avalokita, I went to the temple of the god of love. I saw there a beauteous maid. I have become a victim to her glances. Her gait was stately. Her train bespoke a princely rank. Her garb was graced with youth's appropriate ornaments. Her form was beauty's shrine, or of that shrine she moved as the guardian deity. Whatever Nature offers fairest and best had surely been assembled to mould her charms. Love omnipotent was her creator. Then I too plainly noted that the lovely maid, revealed the signs of passion long entertained for some happy youth.

"Her shape was as slender as the lotus stalk. Her pallid cheeks, like unstained ivory, rivalled the beauty of the spotless moon. I scarcely had gazed upon her, but my eyes felt new delight, as bathed with nectar. She drew my heart at once towards her as powerfully as the magnet does the unresisting iron. That heart, though its sudden passion may be causeless, is fixed on her for ever, chance what may, and though my portion be henceforth despair. The goddess Destiny decrees at pleasure the good or ill of all created beings."

Makranda observes, "Believe me, this cannot be without some cause. Behold! all nature's sympathies spring not from outward form but from inward virtue. The lotus does not bud till the sun has risen. The moon-gem does not melt till it feels the moon." Madhava goes on with his description thus:—

"When her fair train beheld me, they exchanged expressive looks and smiles and murmured to one another as if they knew me. What firmness could resist the honest warmth of nature's mute expressiveness? Those looks of love, beaming with mild timidity and moist with sweet abandonment, tore off my heart,—nay plucked it from my bosom by the roots, all pierced with wounds. Being incredulous of my happiness, I sought to mark her passion, without displaying my own. A stately elephant received the princess and bore her towards the city. Whilst she moved, she shot from her delicate lids retiring glances, tipped with venom and ambrosia, My breast received the shafts. Words cannot paint my agony. Vain were the lunar rays or gelid streams to cool my body's fever, whilst my mind whirls in perpetual round and does not know rest. Requested by Lavangika, I gave her the flowery wreath. She took it with respect, as if it were a precious gift and all the while the eyes of Malati were fixed on her. Bowing with reverence, she than retired."

Makaranda remarks—

"Your story most plainly shows that Malati's affection is your own. The soft cheek, whose pallid tint denoted love pre-conceived, is pale alone for you; She must have seen you. Maidens of her rank do not allow their eyes to rest on one to whom they have not already given their hearts. And then, those looks that passed among her maidens plainly showed the passion you had awakened in their mistress. Then comes her foster-sister's clear enigma and tells intelligibly whose her heart is."

Kalahansa, advancing, shows a picture and says, "This picture is the work of hers who has stolen Madhava's heart. Mandarika gave it to me. She had it from Lavangika, Malati painted it to amuse and relieve distress." Makaranda says, "This lovely maid, the soft light of your eyes, assuredly regards you bound to her in love's alliance. What should prevent your union? Fate and love combined seem labouring to effect it. Come, let me behold the wondrous form that works such change in you. You have the skill. Portray her."

Madhava, in return, delineates the likeness of Malati on the same tablet and Makaranda writes under it the following impassioned love-stanza,

"Whatever nature loveliness displays,
May seem to others beautiful and bright;
But since these charms have broken upon my gaze,
They form my life's sole exquisite delight."

Being asked by Makaranda as to how and where Malati first saw Madhava, Mandarika says, "Malati was called to the lattice by Lavangika to look at him as he passed the palace."

The picture is restored to Mandarika and brought back to Malati.

The mutual passion of the lovers, encouraged by their respective confidants, is naturally increased.

Madhava thus addresses Makaranda,

"It is strange, most strange! wherever I turn, the same loved charms appear on every side. Her beauteous face gleams as brightly as the golden bud of the young lotus. Alas! my friend, this fascination spreads over all my senses. A feverish flame consumes my strength. My heart is all on fire. My mind is tossed with doubt. Every faculty is absorbed in one fond thought.

I cease to be myself or conscious of the thing I am.

Malati thus addresses Lavangika:—

"Love spreads through every vein like subtlest poison and, like fire that brightens in the breeze, consumes this feeble frame.

Resistless fever preys on each fibre. Its fury is fatal. No one can help me. Neither father nor mother nor Lavangika can save me. Life is distasteful to me.

"Repeatedly recurring to the anguish of my heart, I lose all fortitude and in my grief become capricious and unjust. Forgive me. Let the full moon blaze in the mighty sky. Let love rage on. Death screens me from his fury."

In the meantime, the king makes the long-expected demand and the minister Bhurivasu returns the following ambiguous answer:—

"Your Majesty may dispose of your daughter as your Majesty pleases."[1]

The intelligence reaches the lovers. They are thrown into despair.

Requested by Lavangika, Kamandaki thus describes Madhava in the presence of Malati:—

"The sovereign of Vidarbha boasts for minister the wise and long-experienced Devarata, who bears the burden of state and spreads throughout the world his piety and fame. Your father knows him well. For, in their youth, they were joined in study and trained to learning by the same preceptor.

"In this world we rarely behold such characters as theirs. Their lofty rank is the abode of wisdom and of piety, of valour and of virtue. Their fame spreads white and spotless through the universe. A son has sprung from Devarata whose opening virtues early give occasion of rejoicing to the world. Now, in his bloom, this youth has been sent to our city to collect ripe stores of knowledge. His name is Madhava."

Kamandaki soliloquises thus:—

"Malati is tutored to our wishes and inspired with hatred of the bridegroom Nandan. He is reminded of the examples of *Sakuntala* and *Vasavadatta* that vindicate the free choice of a husband. Her admiration of her youthful lover is now approved by his illustrious birth and my encomium of his high descent. All this

---

1   This answer is used in a double sense:—
     "Your minister's daughter is your own daughter and you can dispose of her as you please," and "You can dispose of your own daughter as you please, but not my daughter."
     The father's connivance at his daughter's stolen marriage would appear inconsistent if the reply is not understood in its double sense.

must strengthen and confirm her passion. Now their union may be left to fate."

By the contrivance of Kamandaki, a second interview between the lovers takes place in the public garden of the temple of *Sankara*. Malati is persuaded that the god *Sankara* is to be propitiated with offerings of flowers gathered by one's self. Whilst she is collecting her oblation she and Madhava meet as if by accident.

At this moment, a great tumult and terrific screams announce that a tremendous tiger has escaped from an iron cage in the temple of Siva, spreading destruction everywhere. Instantly, Nandana's youthful sister, Madayantika happens to be passing, and is attacked by the tiger and is reported to be in imminent danger.

Madhava and Makaranda both rush to the rescue. The latter kills the animal, and thus saves her who is then brought in a half-fainting state into the garden. He is himself wounded. Mandayantika is thus saved by the valour of Makaranda. The gallant youth is brought in insensible. By the care of the women, he revives.

On recovering, Madayantika naturally falls in love with her deliverer.

The two couples are thus brought together. Malati affiances herself there and then to Madhava.

Soon afterwards, the king prepares to enforce the marriage of Malati with Nandan. A messenger arrives to summon Madayantika to be present at the marriage. Another messenger summons Malati herself to the king's place.

Madhava is mad with grief and in despair makes the extraordinary resolution of purchasing the aid of ghosts and malignant spirits by going to the cemetery and offering them living flesh, cut off from his own body, as food. He accordingly bathes in the river Sindhu and goes at night to the cemetery. The cemetery happens to be near the temple of the awful goddess Chamunda, a form of Durga. The temple is presided over by a sorceress named Kapalkundla and her preceptor, a terrible necromancer Aghorghanta. They have determined on offering some beautiful maiden as a human victim to the goddess. With this object they carry off Malati, before her departure, while asleep on a terrace and bringing her to the temple, are about to kill her at the shrine when her cries of distress attract the attention of Madhava, who is, at the moment, in the cemetery offering his flesh to the ghosts.

He thinks he recognizes the voice of Malati. He rushes forward to her rescue. She is discovered dressed as a victim and the magician and the sorceress are preparing for the sacrifice.

He encounters Aghorghanta and, after a terrific hand-to-hand fight, kills him and rescues Malati.

She flies to his arms. Voices are heard as of persons in search of Malati. Madhava places her in safety.

The sorceress vows vengeance against Madhava for slaying her preceptor Aghorghanta.

Malati is now restored to her friends. The preparations for Malati's wedding with Nandana goes on. The old priestess Kamandaki, who favours the union of Malati with her lover Madhava, contrives that, by the king's command, the bridal dress shall be put on at the very temple where her own ministrations are conducted.

There she persuades Makaranda to substitute himself for the bride. He puts on the bridal dress, is carried in procession to the house of Nandan and goes through the form of being married to him. Nandana, being disgusted with the masculine appearance of the pretended bride, and offended by the rude reception given to him, vows to have no further communication with her and consigns her to his sister's care in the inner apartments. This enabled Makaranda to effect an interview with Nandana's sister Madayantika, the object of his own affections.

Makaranda then discovers himself to his mistress and persuades her to run away with him to the place where Malati and Madhava have concealed themselves.

Their flight is discovered. The king's guards are sent in pursuit. A great fight follows; but Makaranda, assisted by Madhava, defeats his opponents. The bravery and handsome appearance of the two youths avert the king's anger and they are allowed to join their friends unpunished.

The friends accordingly assemble at the gate of the temple.

But the sorceress, who has been watching an opportunity when Malati is unprotected, takes advantage of the confusion and carries her off in a flying car, in revenge for the death of her preceptor. The distress of her lover and friends knows no bounds. They are reduced to despair at this second obstacle to the marriage. They give up all hopes of recovering her when they are happily relieved by the opportune arrival of Soudamini, an old pupil of the priestess Kamandaki, who has acquired extraordinary magical powers by her penances.

She rescues Malati from the hands of the sorceress and restores her to her despairing lover.

The two couples are now united in happy wedlock.

HANUMAN NATAKA

or

MAHANATAKA

or

THE GREAT DRAMA.

In Ayodhya, there was an illustrious and powerful monarch, the subduer of foes and the renowned ornament of the exalted house of the sun, named Dasaratha in whose family, for the purpose of relieving the Earth of her burden, Bhurisravas (Vishnu) deigned to incorporate his divine substance as four blooming youths. The eldest, endowed with the qualities of imperial worth, was Rama.

He goes with his brother Lakshmana to the court of Mithila, to try his strength in the bending of the bow of Siva, and thereby win Sita for his bride. The hero triumphs. The bow is broken with a deafening sound which brings Parasurama there. Rama wins his bride. He tries the bow of Parasurama and shoots an arrow from it which flies to Swerga or heaven. The Brahmin hero now acknowledges the Kshatriya hero to be his superior. Rama is married to Sita. The sweet loves of the happy pair grows with enjoyment.

Various portents then indicate Rama's impending separation from his father. The sun looks forth dimmed in radiance. Fiery torches wave along the sky. Meteors dart headlong through midheaven. Earth shakes. The firmament rains showers of blood. Around, the horizon thickens. In the day, the pale stars gleam. Unseasonable eclipse darkens the noon. Day echoes with the howls of dogs and jackals, whilst the air replies with horrid and strange sounds, such as shall peal, when the destroying deity proclaims in thunder the dissolution of the world. Rama is exiled. At this, the king dies in agony. It is the result of the stern curse denounced upon the king by the father of the ascetic whom the king, hunting in his youthful days, had accidentally slain.

Rama fixes his residence at Panchavati. Maricha, a Rakshasa, now appears as a deer. The supposed animal is chased by Rama and Lakshmana at Sita's request.

Ravana then comes disguised to see Sita. He mutters, "pious dame! Give me food." She heedlessly oversteps the magic ring traced by Lakshmana, when the Rakshasa seizes her by the hand stretched in charity. She calls in vain the sons of Raghu. Jatayu, the vulture, endeavours to rescue her, but is slain. She encounters Hanuman, the chief Counsellor of Sugriva, the dethroned king of the Monkeys, and begs him to carry her ornaments, which she casts to him, to Rama.

Having slain the deer, the prince, with his brave brother, returns to their bower. He seeks Sita, but seeks in vain. His steps tread three several quarters, the fourth he leaves, overcome with grief and terror, unexplored.

Rama prosecutes his search after Sita. He fights with Bali, the king of the Monkeys, and triumphs over him.

He now despatches Hanuman to Lanka, Hanuman pays a visit to Sita.

He performs various feats at Lanka and returns to Rama whose hosts now advance towards Lanka.

Vibhishana, the brother of Ravana, expostulates with his royal brother, but in vain. Consequently he deserts the king and goes over to Rama.

The Monkeys advance further towards Lanka.

A bridge is built over the sea.

The troops cross over it.

Where first the Monkey bands advance, they view a watery belt smoothly circling round the shore: the following troops plough their way through the thick mire with labour; the chief who leads the rear, filled with wonder, exclaims, "Here is Ocean."

Rama now sends Angada, the son of Bali, to persuade Ravana to relinquish Sita peaceably. Angada has some feeling of aversion to Rama, who killed his father, but thinks he shall best fulfil his father's wishes by promoting the war between Ravana and Rama; he therefore goes to Ravana and defies him in very haughty terms.

Ravana says:—

"Indra, the king of the gods, weaves garlands for me; the thousand-rayed or the Sun keeps watch at my gate; above my head Chandra or the Moon uprears the umbrella of dominion; the wind's and the ocean's monarchs are my slaves; and for my board the fiery godhead toils. Knowest thou not this, and canst thou stoop to praise the son of Raghu, whose frail mortal body is but a meal to any of my households?"

Angada laughs and observes:—"Is this thy wisdom, Ravana? Infirm of judgement dost thou deem of Rama thus—a mortal man? Then Ganga merely flows a watery stream; the elephants that bear the skies, and Indra's steed, are brutal forms; the charms of Rembha are the fleeting beauties of earth's weak daughters, and the golden age, a term of years. Love is a petty archer; the mighty Hanuman, in thy proud discernment, is an ape."

Angada, having in vain endeavoured to persuade Ravana to restore Sita, leaves him to expect the immediate advance of the Monkey host.

Virupaksha and Mahodara, two of Ravana's ministers utter a string of moral and political sentences.

Ravana is not to be persuaded, but goes to Sita to try the effect of his personal solicitations—first endeavouring to deceive her by two fictitious heads, made to assume the likenesses of Rama and Lakshmana. Sita's lamentations are stopped by a heavenly monitor, who tells her that the heads are the work of magic and they instantly disappear. Ravana then vaunts his prowess in war and love, and approaches Sita to embrace her. She exclaims "Forbear, forbear! proud fiend, the jetty arms of my loved lord, or thy relentless sword, alone shall touch my neck."

Thus repulsed, Ravana withdraws, and presently reappears as Rama, with his own ten heads in his hands. Sita, thinking him to be what he appears, is about to embrace him, when the secret virtue of her character as a faithful wife detects the imposition, and reveals the truth to her. Ravana, baffled and mortified, is compelled to relinquish his design. Sita's apprehensions, lest she should be again beguiled, are allayed by a voice from heaven, which announces that she will not see the real Rama until he has beheld Mandodari kiss the dead body of her husband Ravana.

A female Rakhasi attempts to assassinate Rama, but is stopped and slain by Angada. The army then advances to Lanka, and Ravana comes forth to meet it. Kumbhakarna, his gigantic and sleepy brother, is disturbed from his repose to combat. He is rather out of humour at first, and recommends Ravana to give up the lady, observing: "Though the commands of royalty pervade the world, yet sovereigns ever should remember, the light of justice must direct their path." Ravana answers:—

"They who assist us with a holy text are but indifferent friends. These arms have wrested victory from the opposing grasp of gods and demons. Confiding in thy prowess, sure in thee to triumph over my foes, I have relaxed their fibre, but again their nerves are braced, I need thee not; hence to thy cell and sleep." Kumbhakarna replies:—"King, do not grieve, but like a valiant chief, pluck from thy heart all terror of thine enemies, and only deem of thy propitious fortunes, or who shall foremost plunge into the fight——I will not quit thee."

Kumbhakarna's advance terrifies Rama's troops, whom the

Kshatriya hero addresses thus:

"Ho! chiefs and heroes, why this groundless panic, the prowess of our enemy untried in closer conflict? Ocean's myriad fry would drain the fountain, and before the swarm of hostile gnats the mighty lion falls." Kumbhakarna is killed by Rama; on which Indrajit, a son of Ravana, proceeds against the brethren. By the arrow called *Nagapasa*, presented him by Brahma, he casts Rama and Lakshmana senseless on the ground, and then goes to Nikumbhila mountain to obtain a magic car by means of sacrifice. Hanumana disturbs his rites.

Rama and Lakshmana revive, and on being sprinkled with drops of amrita brought by Garura, the latter with a shaft decapitates Meghnada, and tosses the head into the hands of his father Ravana.

Ravana levels a shaft at Lakshmana, given him by Brahma, and charged with the certain fate of one hero. Hanumana snatches it away, after it has struck Lakshmana, before it does mischief. Ravana reproaches Brahma, and he sends Nareda to procure the dart again and keep Hanumana out of the way. With the fatal weapon Lakshmana is left for dead. Rama despairs:—

"My soldiers shall find protection in their caves; I can die with Sita, but thou, Vibhishana, what shall become of thee?"

Hanuman reappears and encourages him. Ravana has a celebrated physician, Sushena, who is brought away from Lanka in his sleep, and directs that a drug (*Vishalya*) from the Druhima mountain must be procured before morning, or Lakshmana will perish. This mountain is six millions of *Yojanas* remote, but Hanuman undertakes to bring it bodily to Lanka, and call at Ayodhya on his way.

He accordingly roots up the mountain, and is returning with it to Rama, via Ayodhya, when Bharata, who is employed in guarding a sacrifice made by Vasishtha, not knowing what to make of him, shoots Hanuman as he approaches. He falls exclaiming on Rama and Lakshmana, which leads Bharata to discover his mistake. Vasishtha restores the monkey who sets off for Lanka. On Hanuman's return, the medicament is administered, and Lakshman revives.

An ambassador from Ravana comes and offers to give up Sita for the battle-axe of Parasurama, but this, Rama replies, must be reserved for Indra. On this refusal, Ravana goes forth after a brief dialogue with his queen Mandodari, who animates his drooping courage with the true spirit of the tribe to which she belongs.

"Banish your sorrow, lord of Lanka, take one long and last

embrace. We meet no more. Or give command, and by your side I march fearless to fight, for I too am a Kshatriya." The progress of Ravana through the air appals all Nature. The winds breathe low in timid murmurs through the rustling woods; the sun with slackened fires gleams pale abroad and the streams, relaxing from their rapid course, slowly creep along. Ravana defies Rama with great disdain and in derision of his modest demeanour, asks him whether he is not overcome with shame by the recollection of his ancestor, Anaranya, killed formerly by Ravana.

Rama replies:—

"I am not ashamed my noble ancestor fell in the combat. The warrior seeks victory or death, and death is not disgrace. It ill befits thee to revile his fame. When vanquished, thou couldst drag out an abject life in great Haihaya's dungeons, till thy sire begged thee to freedom, as a matter of charity. For thee alone I blush, unworthy of my triumph."

Ravana falls under the arrows of Rama. The heads, that once, sustained on Siva's breast, shone with heavenly splendour, now lie beneath the vulture's talons. Mandodari bewails the death of her husband. Sita is recovered, but Rama is rather shy of his bride, until her purity is established by her passing through the fiery ordeal: a test she successfully undergoes. Rama returns with Sita and his friends to Ayodhya, when Angada challenges them all to fight him, as it is now time to revenge his father's death. A voice from heaven, however, tells him to be pacified, as Bali will be born as hunter in a future age, and kill Rama, who will then be Krishna: he is accordingly appeased. Rama is now seated on the throne of Ayodhya. After some time, he orders the exile of Sita.

ANERGHA RAGHAVA

or

MURARI NATAKA

The sage Viswamitra comes to Dasaratha, the king of Ayodhya, to request the aid of his eldest son Rama. Each tries to outdo the other in complimentary speeches. The sage observes:—

"The monarch of the day invests the dawn with delegated rays to scatter night, and ocean sends his ministers the clouds, to shed his waters over the widespread earth."

The king, taking counsel with himself, and being reminded by Vamadeva, one of his priests and preceptors, that the race of Raghu never sent away a petitioner ungratified, sends for Rama and Lakshmana, and allows Viswamitra to take them with him, to his hermitage, situated on the banks of the Kausiki or Coosy river, to protect him in his rites against the oppression of Taraka, a Rakshasi.

The cry is heard that Taraka is abroad. Rama, after some hesitation about killing a female, slays her.

Viswamitra now proposes that they should visit Mithila. The two princes are introduced to Janaka, the king of Mithila, who is urged by the sage to let Rama try to bend the bow of Siva. Sanshkala, the messenger of Ravana, the king of Lanka, now arrives to demand Sita in marriage for his master, refusing, at the same time, on his part, to submit to the test of bending the bow. The demand is refused. Rama tries his fortune, bends the bow and wins the lady. The family connection is extended by the promise of Urmila, Mandavi, and Srutakirti, to Rama's brothers. Sanshkala is highly indignant and carries the information to his master's minister Malyavan, who is disappointed on Ravana's account. Malyavan anticipates that Ravana will carry Sita off; and to render the attempt less perilous, projects inveighing Rama into the forests alone, for which he sends Surpanakha, the sister of Ravana, in the disguise of Manthara, the attendant of Kaukeyi.

Parasurama then appears and boasts of his destruction of the Kshatriya race. Rama replies:—"This flag of your fame is now worn to tatters, let us see if you can mount a new one." Rama then calls for his bow, and Parasurama presents him with his axe. They go forth to fight. In the end, the two Ramas turn very excellent friends. Parasurama departs.

Dasaratha now declares his purpose of relinquishing the

kingdom entirely to his son Rama, Lakshmana announces the arrival of Manthara, and presents a letter from Kaikeyi, the purpose of which is to urge Dasaratha's fulfilment of his promise, and grant her as the two boons, the Coronation of Bharata, and banishment of Rama. The old king faints. Rama recommending his father to Janaka, departs for the forests, accompanied by Lakshmana and Sita. On their arrival in the forests, they are cordially received by Sugriva, the brother of Bali the king of the monkeys. Lakshmana carries on a dialogue with Ravana, disguised as a juggler.

Jatayu, the king of birds, beholds Sita carried off by Ravana. He follows the ravisher. Rama and Lakshmana both express their grief.

Lakshmana observes:—

"The worse the ill that Fate inflicts on noble souls, the more their firmness; and they arm their spirits with adamant to meet the blow."

Rama replies:—

"The firmness I was born with or was reared to, and rage, that fills my heart, restrain my sorrows; but hard is the task to fit my soul to bear unmurmuringly a husband's shame."

A cry of distress is now heard, and on looking out, the youths observe Guha, the friendly forest monarch, assailed by the demon Kabandha, or a fiend without a head. Lakshmana goes to his aid, and returns with his friend Guha. In the act of delivering him, Lakshmana tosses away the skeleton of Dundubhi, a giant, suspended by Bali, who, deeming this an insult, presently appears. After a prolix interchange of civility and defiance, Rama and Bali resolve to determine their respective supremacy by single combat. Bali is slain. His brother Sugriva is inaugurated as king and determines to assist Rama to recover Sita. A bridge is built over the sea. Rama's army advance to Lanka. Kumbhakarna, a brother of Ravana, and Meghanada, a son of Ravana, go forth to battle. Malyavan wishes them prosperity in a phrase perfectly oracular. They are slain. Ravana now takes the field himself. Malyavan resolves to follow him and resign, on the sword, a life now useless to his sovereign. The king is overthrown. Sita is recovered.

Rama with his wife and brother, accompanied by Vibhishana, the brother of Ravana, and Sugriva, mounts the celestial car, which was once wrested by Ravana from his brother Kuvera, and sets out to proceed to Ayodhya.

On the way the travellers descry the Sumeru mountain, the Malaya mountain, the Dandaka forest, the mountain Prasravana, the Godaveri river, mount Malyavan, Kundinipura in the Maharashtra country, the shrine of Bhimeswara, the city of Kanchi, Ujayin, the temple of Mahakala, Mahishmati the capital of Chedi, the Jumna and Ganga rivers, Varanasi, Mithila or Tirhut, and Champa near Bhagalpur.

They then proceed westward to Prayaga, and Antarvedi or Doab, when they again follow an easterly course and arrive at Ayodhya.

Bharata, Satrughna, Vasishtha the priest and the people of Ayodhya await the arrival of the party and receive them most cordially. Rama is now crowned king.

VENI SAMVARANA

or

VENI SANHARA

or

"THE BINDING OF THE BRAID OF HAIR"

Draupadi, the wife of the Pandavas, is dragged by the *veni* or braid of hair into the public assembly by the hand of Duhsasana, one of the Kaurava princes, a disgrace that weighs most heavily upon the Pandavas, who contemplate most bitter revenge.

Krishna returns to the Pandava camp from a visit to the Kaurava princes, as a mediator between the contending chiefs. Ferocious Bhima expresses, to his brother Sahadeva, his refusal to have any share in the negotiations instituted by Krishna and his determination to make no peace with the enemy until the insult offered to Draupadi is avenged. He announces his resolution, in case the dispute be amicably adjusted, to disclaim all connection with his own brothers, and throw off obedience to Judhishthira.

The price of peace is the demand of five villages or towns, Indraprastha, Tilaprastha, Mansadam, Varanavatam, and another. Sahadeva attempts to calm the fury of Bhima, but in vain; and Draupadi, with her hair still dishevelled, and pining over her ignominious treatment, comes to inflame his resentment. She complains also of a recent affront offered by Bhanumati, the queen of Duryodhana, in an injurious comment upon her former exposure, which serves to widen the breach.

Krishna's embassy is unsuccessful, and he effects his return only by employing his divine powers against the enemy. All the chiefs are summoned by the trumpet to prepare for battle.

Before day-break, Bhanumati repeats, to her friend and an attendant, a dream in which she has beheld a *Nakula* or Mungoose destroy a hundred snakes. This is very ominous, *Nakula* being one of the Pandavas, and the sons of Kuru amounting to a hundred. Duryodhana overhears part of the story, and at first imagines the hostile prince is the hero of the vision. He is about to burst upon her, full of rage, and when he catches the true import of the tale, he is at first disposed to be alarmed by it, but at last wisely determines to disregard it.

For, by Angira it is sung, the aspect of the planets, dreams and signs, meteors and portents, are the sports of accident, and do not move the wise. Bhanumati offers an *arghya* of sandal and flowers to the rising sun to avert the ill omen, and then the king appears and soothes her.

Their dialogue is disturbed by a rising whirlwind from which they take shelter in a neighbouring pavilion. The mother of Jayadratha, the king of Sindhu, then appears, and apprises Duryodhana that Arjuna has vowed, if sunset finds Jayadratha alive, he will sacrifice himself in the flames. His wrath is especially excited by the death of his son Abhimanyu, in which that chieftain had borne a leading part. Duryodhana laughs at her fears and those of his wife, and despises the resentment of the Pandavas. He observes, that this was fully provoked by the treatment which Draupadi received by his command, when in the presence of the court and of the Pandavas, she called out in vain for mercy. Duryodhana then orders his war-chariot and goes forth to the battle. Up to the period of the contest, the following chiefs have fallen, Bhagadatta, Sindhuraja, Angadhipa, Drupada, Bhurisravas, Somadatta, and Bahlika.

Ghatotkacha is also slain, and Bhima is about to avenge his fall, on which account Hirimba, the queen of the Rakshasas and mother of Ghatotkacha, has ordered goblins to be ready to assist Bhimasena.

Drona is seized by Dhrishtadyumna and slain. Aswatthama, the son of Drona, appears armed and is overtaken by his father's charioteer who tells him of the treachery by which Drona was slain, having been induced to throw away his arms by a false report that his son Aswatthama had perished, and been then killed at a disadvantage. Aswatthama's distress is assuaged by his maternal uncle Kripa, who recommends him to solicit the command of the host from Duryodhana.

In the meantime, proud Kerna, the friend and ally of Duryodhana, fills the mind of the Kuru chief with impressions hostile to Drona and his son, persuading him that Drona only fought to secure Aswatthama's elevation to royal dignity, and that he threw away his life, not out of grief, but in despair at the disappointment of his ambitious schemes. Kripa and Aswatthama now arrive and Duryodhana professes to condole with Aswatthama for his father's loss. Kerna sneeringly asks him what he purposes, to which he replies:—

"Whoever confident in arms is ranked amongst the adverse host—whomever the race of proud Panchala numbers, active youth, weak age or unborn babes, whoever beheld my father's murder, or whoever dares to cross my path, shall fall before my vengeance. Dark is my sight with rage, and Death himself, the world's destroyer, should not escape my fury."

Kripa then requests Duryodhana to give the command of the army to Aswatthama. The king excuses himself on the plea of having promised it to Kerna, to whom he transfers his ring accordingly. A violent quarrel ensues between Kerna and Aswatthama, and Duryodhana and Kripa have some difficulty in preventing them from single combat. Fiery Aswatthama at last reproaches Duryodhana with partiality, and refuses to fight for him more. Bhima proclaims that he has at last encountered Duhsasana, the insulter of Draupadi, and is about to sacrifice him to his vengeance. Kerna, instigated by Aswatthama, foregoes his anger and is about to resume his arms when a voice from heaven prevents him. He is obliged, therefore, to remain an idle spectator of the fight, but desires Kripa to assist the king. They go off to fight.

Duhsasana is killed and the army of the Kauravas is put to the rout. Duryodhana is wounded and becomes insensible. On his recovery, he hears of Duhsasana's death and gives vent to his sorrows.

In the conflict between Arjuna and Vrishasena, the son of Kerna, the young prince is slain to his father's distress. Sundaraka, a follower of Kerna, brings a leaf on which Kerna has written to Duryodhana, with an arrow dipped in his own blood, message for aid. Duryodhana orders his chariot, and prepares to seek the fight again, when he is prevented by the arrival of his parents, Dhritarashtra and Gandhari, who with Sanjaya, endeavour to prevail upon Duryodhana to sue for peace, but he refuses.

A tumult and the entrance of the king's charioteer announce the death of Kerna. Duryodhana, after expressing his grief, determines to go and avenge him, and mount the car of Sanjaya, the charioteer of Dhritarashtra, for that purpose, when Arjuna and Bhima arrive in search of him.

On finding the seniors there, Arjuna purposes to withdraw; but Bhima insists on first addressing them, which they do, but in insulting terms.

Dhritarashtra, reproaching them for this language, is told they use it not in pride, but in requital of his having witnessed, without interfering to prevent, the oppression and barbarous treatment the Pandavas experienced from his sons. Duryodhana interferes and defies Bhima, who is equally anxious for the combat; but Arjuna prevents it, and the brothers are called off by a summons from Yudhishthira, who orders the battle to cease for the day and the dead bodies of either party to be burnt. Aswatthama is now disposed to be reconciled to Duryodhana; but the prince receives his advances coldly, and he withdraws in disgust. Dhritarashtra sends Sanjaya after him to persuade him to overlook Duryodhana's conduct. Duryodhana mounts his car, and the aged couple seek the tent of Salya, the king of Madra.

Duryodhana is discovered concealed in a swamp, and compelled to fight with Bhimasena, by whom he is slain. Yudhisthira orders public rejoicings on the occasion.

Charvaka, a Rakshasa disguised as a sage, then enters, requiring rest and water. He relates that he has seen Arjuna engaged with Duryodhana, Bhima having been previously slain by the latter, and gives his hearers to understand that Arjuna also has fallen. Draupadi determines to mount the funeral pile, and Yudhishthira, to put an end to himself when the Rakshasa, satisfied with the success of his scheme, which was intended to prevail on this couple to perish, departs. The pile is prepared, and Yudhishthira and Draupadi are about to sacrifice themselves, when they are disturbed by a great clamour. Supposing it to precede the approach of Duryodhana, Yudhishthira calls for his arms, when Bhima, his club besmeared with blood, rushes in. Draupadi runs away; he catches her by the hair, and is seized by Yudhishthira— on which the mistake is discovered.

The braid of Draupadi's hair is now again bound up. Arjuna and Vasudeva arrive, and announce that they have heard of the fraud of Charvaka. On hearing that the mendicant is slain by Nakula, Krishna expresses great satisfaction.

CHANDA KAUSIKA

or

THE OFFENDED VISWAMITRA

Maharaja Harischandra, a scion of the solar race, a powerful king, endowed with uncommon virtues and skilled in all arts, sees a vision of misfortune to come. Apprehending future evils for his subjects, he confers with his priest, and acting on his advice, spends a whole night in religious contemplation in a temple of God. Next morning the king enters the inner apartments of his palace to greet his wife. The queen, who is jealous on account of his absence during the night, says to him, "Oh! I see your eyes are red for want of sleep. The sight is not uninteresting; only, I am being consumed with the fires of agony of mind." The king, on hearing this, smiles and says, "Oh my dear queen! do not be angry. Be assured, you have no rival in Harischandra's affections".

The queen is not altogether satisfied with this assurance, for love is suspicious. Just then, a messenger comes to request permission to bring in a hermit who is standing at the door. The permission is granted and the hermit enters. Addressing the King, he says, "The family priest has sent you some holy water, which will bring you peace of mind and ward off the evils for fear of which he made you keep up a whole night." The king and the queen thankfully accept the water. The hermit retires. The queen, now learning from the hermit the cause of her husband's absence from her, and of his wakefulness all night, becomes ashamed of herself and asks her lord's pardon for the false insinuation she had made. On this he kisses the queen.

Again, the king goes on a hunting expedition. Hunting is a favourite pastime with kings. It promotes health and courage and gives immense pleasure to all who engage in it. When the king enters a thick forest, he finds the great sage Viswamitra deeply engaged in religious austerities with the view of acquiring the three unattainable arts of creation, preservation and destruction, which properly belong to Brahma, Vishnu and Siva respectively. The gods plot to prevent this consummation, and send a servant named Bighna. Bighna assumes the form of a boar and appears before the king. The king discharges an arrow at him, but in vain. The animal enters the thick forest. The king follows. It now enters the hermitage of Viswamitra. The king addresses his followers thus, "It is the duty of kings to get rid of carnivorous animals from the forest of meditation and austerities. I have, on the contrary, made a carnivorous animal enter it. How can I now retire? But the hermits will be disturbed in their religious exercises if you all enter. So, do you all wait here. I will proceed alone." With these observations, the king enters the forest of meditation and is charmed with its exquisite beauty.

The king thinks, "Tearing off the bonds of the world is the cause of hermits' ease and happiness. With no attachments, no desires, no bereavements, no worldly anxieties, they are happily absorbed in divine contemplation." The king is thinking thus when distant cries are heard, as if females are crying out, "Maharaja Harischandra! save us! save us! Save us from the fire-place of this mighty hermit. We three helpless women are being burnt up."

At this, the king is at a loss. His heart melts at the tender cries of the women. He extinguishes the flame with his weapon dedicated to Varuna, the god of the waters.

The three ladies are the three arts of creation, preservation and destruction. They, thus delivered, go away to Heaven, showering blessings of victory on their deliverer.

The meditations of the dreadful sage Viswamitra are thus broken off. His eyes are red with anger. Seeing Harischandra standing before him he cries out, "Oh wretch of a Kshattriya! I will burn you up as Siva did the god of love."

The king is at a loss. He trembles as a plantain tree tossed up by tempest. He touches the feet of the sage and most piteously begs pardon of him.

But the sage is obdurate. He will not be appeased. He is about to consume the offender with imprecation.

The Raja again and again implores him thus:—

"My lord Kausika! Forgive me. I was touched by the piteous appeals of the women and disturbed you for the sake of duty."

At this, the sage becomes still more furious and says trembling, "O Villain! speak of duty! What is your duty?"

The king replies,

"O god! gifts to virtuous Brahmans, protection of those afflicted with fear, and fight with enemies are the three chief duties of Kshattriyas."

The sage thereupon observes,

"If compliance with duties be your aim, make some gift to me commensurate with my merit."

The king replies, "Oh great sage! what have I got with which to make a due gift to you? I am prepared to give you what I have——this world with all its wealth. Please accept it."

Then the sage becomes calm and says,

"Be it so. I will not burn you up. I accept your gift of a kingdom. Now that you have made a gift, give me a fee of one thousand gold coins, commensurate with the gift. I will not accept the gift without the fee. But as you have made a gift of the world with all its wealth, you must not take the fee-money out of that world. Collect the money elsewhere."

At this, the king is in a fix. After much thought it strikes him that it is said in the scriptures that Benares is separate from the world. So he resolves to collect money from that holy city.

Then the king placing the crown and the sceptre of royalty at the feet of the sage, obtains from him one month's time to pay the fee and taking the queen Saibya and his son Rohitasya with him, starts for Benares. The month allowed him is drawing to a close. Not a single gold coin has been collected—to say nothing of one thousand coins. Alms is the only way of collection. Alms barely suffices for maintenance. On the morning of the last day, when he is deeply anxious for the money, the sage arrives. Seeing the latter, he almost faints.

The sage whirls his eyes and asks, "Oh Harischandra! where is my fee? Pay at once, or I will burn you up." He replies in piteous and trembling tones, "The month will be completed by sunset. Please wait till sunset."

The sage observes, "I will not listen to any more of your prevarications. I cannot grant your request."

The king cries and repeatedly entreats the sage to wait till sunset.

At this the queen and his son both weep.

After many entreaties, the sage consents. Then the king again goes out a-begging, but in vain. Then he resolves to sell his person and goes about hawking himself in the streets.

No one responds to his efforts. No buyer appears. At this time, a Brahmin with a disciple, asks whether a male or a female slave is for sale and intimates that he requires a female slave.

The queen wipes her eyes and replies, "Yes, a female slave is for sale for fifty thousand gold coins. I, who am for sale as such, will obey all orders except eating table-refuse and indulging in improper intimacy with males." The Brahmin consents to the terms laid down, pays the required sum into the hands of the king and takes away the queen. The king then bewails her thus:—

"It were far better if a thousand thunderbolts had fallen on my head. Oh my dear queen! Never even in a dream did I think that such a misfortune would befall you. You mistook a poisonous tree for a sandal-tree. Oh, how hard is my heart! It does not melt at the sight of my wife sold away as a slave. Even iron is melted by fire. Oh Providence! I can no longer bear up my sorrows. Oh Indra I break my head in pieces by thy thunderbolts."

At this lamentation of the king, all present become sorry and express their regrets. After a little while, the sage arrives again, his body emitting sparks of fire. Seeing him at a distance, the king begins to tremble.

As the sage comes up, the king bows to him and says,

"My lord Kausika! I have procured only a half of your fee by the sale of my wife. Accept it. I shall presently pay the remaining half by the sale of my own person."

The sage whirls his eyes and exclaims, "Is it a joke? Am I a fit object for a joke? What shall I do with only half the money? Just pay down the whole amount. See the sun is setting."

The king replies, "O God! if this does not satisfy you, I pray you wait a little. If a Chandal is available, I will sell my person to him and pay your fee." The sage remarks:—

"Then I will stand here and wait. Collect the money without delay."

The king then hawks himself about, "Will any one buy me with half a lakh of gold coins, and deliver me from an ocean of sorrows." No one responds to his offer. No buyer appears. The sun is about to set. Death stares him in the face. Not that he fears death. Why should he fear it? He has given away his kingdom. His queen has been sold. Life has no further attraction for him. Death has been stripped of its terrors. But death by the fire of a Brahmin's anger leads to everlasting hell. He sees the vision of hell, falls down on the ground like a plantain tree blown by a tempest, and faints.

Virtue preserves him who practises virtue. Virtue assumes the form of a Chandal and accompanied by an attendant, makes his appearance, with a half-burnt bamboo on his shoulders and a chain of skeletons round his neck. He is ready to buy the king, who now weeps bitterly, and holding the feet of the sage, entreats him thus:—

"Oh lord Kausika! Do me a favour I pray you. Do not sell me to a Chandal. Do *you* rather buy me. I shall be your slave for ever."

On this, the sage flies into a rage and exclaims:—

"Oh villain! Do not trifle with me. You have all this time been pretending that you want buyers. As soon as a buyer appears in the field, you feel ashamed to be sold to a Chandal! I cannot brook any more delay. I take up water to destroy you."

The king begs his pardon, sells himself to the Chandal and pays down the fee to the sage, who then retires.

The king now puts on the dress of a Chandal and is appointed with two others to collect rags in a burning-ground. Hideous is the burning-ground. Dogs and jackals are tearing up carcasses which lie scattered all round. Vultures are quarrelling among themselves. These sights unloosen the bonds that bind him to the world. The king is trembling with fear. His two colleagues have left him. But he will not leave his station. He must do his duty. The night deepens. The burning-ground becomes still more hideous. To try the king's sense of duty, Virtue once more becomes incarnate and this time appears before the king in a horrible form. The king has never before seen such a terrible sight, but still he will not leave his station. Not one or two but myriads of such forms dance before him, but in vain. The king exclaims, "No one shall be allowed to burn any corpse without depositing rags and couches with me. I am the agent of the lord of this burning-ground. I make this proclamation by order of my lord."

No one responds. No voice is heard; only horrible figures are seen playing around him. After a while, a hermit comes and says.

"I am a hermit. I have resolved to practise some *mantras*. I have come to know everything about you by my powers of *yoga*. You are a king and you should protect me from the demons that disturb my meditations."

The king most humbly submits, "My body is not my own; I have sold it to the lord of the Chandals. How can I forsake my duty to my lord to save you?"

The hermit says, "come and help me if I ever suffer extreme distress."

The king replies, "If I can ever help you without detriment to the business of my lord, I am ready to do it." The hermit retires, and after a short time he returns; and says,

"By your help I am now versed in all *mantras*. I am prepared to give you such a mantra as by its virtue you will be able at once to repair to Heaven. You need not suffer hell by slavery to a Chandal."

The king replies, "Many thanks for your kind offer. But how can I accept your offer as this body belongs to a Chandal? I will not go anywhere before death."

The hermit says, "Then take this money and deliver your wife."

The king thankfully declines the offer with the observation, "I have sold my queen in my hour of need. To buy her back is not in my power." The hermit soliloquizes,

"Blessed is Maharaja Harischandra! What fortitude! what wisdom! what generosity! what a sense of duty! The world has never produced a nobler man. A tempest shakes even the mountains, but behold! this noblest specimen of humanity is not moved by the severest of afflictions!

It is morning. The birds are singing. The sun is up in the horizon. The king is sitting on the banks of the Ganges. He is thinking of his fate when he hears a female voice crying. He approaches the lady. The scene is horrible. An unfortunate lady, the queen Saibya who had been deserted by her husband, has come to burn her son, the support of her life. She was serving as a slave in the house of the Brahmin who had bought her. Her son Rohitashya, was stung by a deadly poisonous snake. No body would help her. She has come to the burning-ground to burn the dead body of her son. The queen weeps and faints. The king stares at the face of the corpse for a long time and at last recognises his dead son. He too faints. After a long time he recovers, and finds that the queen also has recovered. He thinks of committing suicide, but the body is not his own. He thinks of pacifying the queen by introducing himself, but his present costume will perhaps aggravate her sorrows. The queen, looking up to the skies, exclaims; "It is high time for me to return to the house of my master. I forget I am a slave. My master will be angry if I am late. My husband will incur blame if my master is angry. Let me go at once."

The king reflects, "If my queen is so mindful of her duties to her master in the midst of such calamities, I must never forget my duty to my master."

Then he approaches the queen and addresses her thus:—

"Who are you? You are not allowed to burn the corpse before you give up its clothes to me, the slave of the lord of this place." She replies,

"Please wait a little. I will take off the clothes."

As the queen delivers the clothes into the hands of the slave, she notices signs of royalty in his hands and is surprised that such a hand is engaged in so low an office.

"She looks attentively and exclaims in a wild voice, Oh my lord! Oh Maharaja! you a slave in this burning-ground! Oh lord Kausika! are you not yet satisfied?" The queen rushes to embrace the king. The king starts away from her and forbids her saying, "Oh my queen! do not touch me, I am the slave of a Chandal. Be patient." She faints again.

The king cannot touch her as he is in the garb of a Chandal. After a while, the queen recovers, and the king addresses her thus:—

"Oh my lady! Abandon lamentations. It is useless to lament. All this is the result of work in previous lives. I will prepare a funeral pyre. Apply the sacrament of fire to the dead body and return at once to the house of your master." The queen is disconsolate and wants to remain with her husband, who explains the situation thus:—"You have no right to remain here. Do not forget that your person has been sold to the Brahmin."

The queen understands and sighs.

All on a sudden, flowers are showered on their heads from Heaven, and musical voices are heard on high proclaiming.

"Blessed is Maharaja Harischandra; Blessed is Rani Shaibya! unrivalled in this world is the liberality, the patience, the resolution and the wisdom of the king. No nobler man can be found in the three worlds."

The king and the queen stare motionless towards the Heavens.

Now virtue assumes the form of a hermit and makes this address.

"Victory to Maharaja Harischandra! You have astonished the world, I am virtue incarnate. Virtue is never vain. As you have stuck to me all along, I must reward you. I will send you to the heaven of *Brahma*, where the greatest kings cannot enter by their truth, charity, straightforwardness and sacrifices. You need not lament any more. Be patient. By my blessing, your son Rohitashya will instantly regain life". Rohitashya now starts up.

Then the king perceives, in clear vision acquired by the blessings of Virtue, that lord Kausika, in order to try his virtue, deprived him of his kingdom and placed the government in the hands of his own minister. The Chandal, who is his master, is not a real character but virtue incarnate.

The Brahmin and his wife, who were the master and mistress of the queen, were not ordinary persons. The Brahmin was Siva, the god of gods, incarnate. The Brahmani was the goddess Durga incarnate. By order of virtue, the king and queen annoint, on the banks of the Ganges, Rohitashya as king-associate or Yuvaraja, and return to the capital, amidst the wild rejoicings of the subjects.

After a short stay there, the happy couple repair to the heaven of *Brahma*.

MADHURANIRUDDHA

The secret loves of Usha, the daughter of the Asura Bana, and Aniruddha, the grandson of Krishna, are intense. The sage Nareda apprises Krishna and Balarama, that Indra is again in dread of the demons, and especially of Bana, who has acquired the particular favour of Siva, and who is therefore not to be easily subdued. The conference ends by Nareda's going to Sonapur, the capital of the demon, to endeavour to impair the friendship between Bana and Siva, whilst Krishna and his brother await the result.

The excessive arrogance of Bana, in his anxiety to match himself with Vishnu, has offended the latter, who has accordingly departed for Kailas, after announcing that Bana's anxiety shall be alleviated whenever his banner falls. Parvati has also gone to Kailas, after announcing to Usha that she will shortly behold her lover. Usha is impatient for the boon conferred by the goddess.

Aniruddha is violently enamoured of a damsel he has seen in his sleep, and despairs of discovering who she is, when Nareda comes opportunely to his aid, and informs him that she is the daughter of Bana; on which Aniruddha determines to go to his capital, first propitiating Jwalamukhi by penance, in order to obtain the means of entering a city surrounded by a wall of perpetual flame. The goddess is the form of Durga, worshipped wherever a subterraneous flame breaks forth, or wherever jets of carburetted hydrogen gas are emitted from the soil.

Bana's banner has fallen. His minister and wife endeavour to prevail on him to propitiate Siva, in order to avert the evil omen, but he refuses.

Bringi, a servant of Durga, precedes Aniruddha to prepare the goddess to grant his request. As he proceeds in his aerial car, he notices the countries of Orissa, Bengal, Behar, Oude or Ayodhya, Prayaga, Hastinapur or Delhi and Kurujangal or Tahneser, whence he comes to Jwalamukhi.

Aniruddha repairs to the shrine of the goddess round which goblins sport, and upon the point of offering himself as a sacrifice, is prevented by the goddess and receives from her the power of travelling through the air.

Usha and Chitralekha, her companion, receive a visit from Nareda, in whose presence the latter unfolds a picture containing portraits of all the chief characters in Swerga, Patala, and on earth, or Indra, and other gods; Sesha, Takshaka and the Nagas, and different princes, as the kings of Magadha, Mathura, Avanti, Madra,

Mahishmati, and Viderbha, Yudhishthira, Krishna, Baladeva, Pradyumna, and finally Aniruddha, whom Usha recognizes as the individual seen in her dream, and of whom she is enamoured. Nareda recommends that Chitralekha be sent to Dwaravati to invite Aniruddha, whom he enables to fly thither, whilst he remains in charge of Usha, whom he sends to the garden to await her lover's arrival.

Aniruddha and Chitralekha arrive at Sonapur and the former is united to his mistress.

Aniruddha is detected by Bana. An engagement ensues. Krishna, Baladeva, and Pradyumna coming to the aid of the prince, the day is going ill with Bana, when Kartikeya, Ganesha, and Siva and Chandi come to his succour. Notwithstanding the presence of his allies, Bana has all his thousand arms cut off by Krishna except four. Siva advances to the aid of his votary, when a combat ensues between the gods which combat Brahma descends to arrest. The gods embrace one another. Parvati and Brahma support Bana to make his submission.

Vishnu declares he is less sensible of the wounds inflicted by Bana, than of the regret he feels at his presumption in contending with Siva. The latter consoles him by telling him he only did a warrior's duty, and that military prowess is independent of all motives of love or hatred.

Parvati then brings Usha to the spot, and by her desire, and that of Siva, Bana gives his daughter to Aniruddha. Siva then elevates him to the rank of one of his attendants, under the name of Mahakala.

SRIDAMA CHARITA

Poverty and Folly are sent by Lakshmi, the goddess of wealth, to assail Sridama, the early companion and fellow-student of Krishna, who has become obnoxious to the goddess for his attachment to Saraswati; the goddess of learning. They effect their purpose with Sridama, by demanding the rites of hospitality, and being accordingly admitted into his dwelling.

Sridama is persuaded by his wife, Vasumati, who has seen a propitious dream, to repair to Krishna, to see if his opulent friend will restore his broken fortunes. He takes with him a handful of rice, dried and cleaned after boiling, as a present. He arrives at the palace of Krishna, where he is received with great respect by the host and his two principal wives, Rukmini and Satyabhama; the former washes his feet, the latter wipes them, and Krishna sprinkles the remaining water upon his own head. After recalling some of the occurrences of their juvenile days, when they were fellow-students, Krishna leads his friend into the garden, where they remain till towards sunset; when they are summoned to join the queens and their attendants. Krishna indulges in frolics among his women. The buffoonery of the Vidushaka amuses the party.

After some time spent in this manner, Sridama takes his leave, and although dismissed with great reverence, departs as poor as he came. He recollects this on his way back, and consoles himself with observing that wealth intoxicates as well as wine, and that the affection of Krishna is a thing which no one can steal from him. His disciple is not so submissive, and reminds him that it was not to get mere civility that he was sent on this errand by his wife.

On arrival, they find, instead of the miserable hovel of Sridama, a splendid and extensive town, and that Sridama is in great affliction at the disappearance of his wife, when he is seen and solicited by a *Kanchuli* or chamberlain, who calls himself his servant, to enter a stately palace. Sridama, thinking this is a jest upon his poverty, threatens to beat him if he does not depart, but the chamberlain perseveres, and tells him that while he was absent, Krishna had converted his cottage into a town, named after him Sridamapur, and supplied it with every article of use or luxury. With much reluctance and unyielding incredulity Sridama is prevailed upon to enter the palace, where he finds his wife.

Krishna now comes to pay a visit to his friend. He arrives in his aerial chariot, accompanied by Satyabhama and the Vidushaka. His bounties are heartily acknowledged by the object on whom they have been bestowed.

KANSA BADHA

or

THE DESTRUCTION OF KANSA

Kansa, the king of Mathura, alarmed by a voice from heaven, that Krishna, the son of his sister, predestined to destroy him, has escaped the precautions taken against him, consults with his minister what he shall do.

The juvenile Krishna performs many exploits. He accomplishes the destruction of the demon Kesi, one of those infernal beings who in vain attempted to kill the divine child, instigated by their prescience of their fate when he should reach maturity.

Akrura, the paternal uncle of Krishna, repairs to Gokul to invite his nephew to Mathura. Balarama and Krishna, after bowing to their foster parents, Nanda and Yasoda and receiving their benedictions, depart for Mathura.

The seniors then express their grief for their loss. While the boys are proceeding on their journey, they are overtaken by a messenger from Radha, in consequence of which Krishna determines to spend some time at Vrindavan. They resume their journey to Mathura. On the way, the youths kill the royal elephant of Kansa. Then they defeat and slay Kansa's two wrestlers Chanura and Mushtika. These occurrences are reported to Kansa. The youths now reach his palace at Mathura and slay him. The boys are then re-united with their mortal parents Vasudeva and Devaki. To console Devaki for her brother's death, Krishna installs her father Ugrasena in the sovereignty of Mathura.

YAYATI CHARITRA

Sermishtha was the daughter of Vrishaperva, king of the Daityas, and Devayani, the daughter of Sukra, regent of the planet Venus and the spiritual preceptor of the Daitya race. Devayani having incurred the displeasure of Sermishtha the latter threw the former into a well, where she was found by king Yayati, the son of Nahusha. Devayani, on returning to her father, excited his anger against Vrishaperva, who, to appease Sukra, consented to give his daughter to Devayani as her servant, with a thousand other female attendants. Devayani was married to Yayati. At the time of her marriage, Sukra obtained the king's promise that he would never associate with Sermishtha; but after some interval, the king meeting her, fell in love with, and espoused, her privately. The intrigue continued secret, until Yayati had two sons by Devayani and three by Sermishtha, when it was discovered by the former, and excited her resentment as well as that of her father. The violation of the king's promise was punished by premature decay, as denounced upon him by Sukra, with permission, however, to transfer his infirmities to anyone who would acccept them. Yayati appealed to his sons; of whom the youngest alone, Puru, consented to assume the burden. After a sufficient period, Yayati took his decrepitude back again, and left the sovereignty to Puru in reward of his filial piety.

All the sons of Yayati were the founders of distinguished families. The Pauravas were the descendants of Puru in whose line the Kaurava and the Pandava families were comprised.

KAUTUKA SERVASWA

Kalivatsala, or the darling of the age of iniquity, is the sovereign of Dhermanasa or the destruction of virtue, and he takes as his spiritual guide, Kukermapanchanana, the Siva of iniquity.

Satyacharya, a pious Brahman returned from Brindavan, who is treated by the king and his courtiers with great iniquity, holds the following conversation with his brethren in jail.

Satyacharya says: "How now, holy sirs, how fares it with you?"

The Brahmans in jail reply: "We once had lands in free gifts."

Satyacharya asks, "What then?"

The Brahmans answer: "why, know you not the customs of the country? If the god of wealth owned lands here that yielded but a grain of corn, the king would send him in three days to beg alms, clad in tatters and with a platter in his hand. The characteristics of our sovereign are fondness for the intoxicating juice of *bhang*, esteem for the wicked, addiction to vice, and detestation of virtue."

Satyacharya observes: "You are right, what chance is there for the good? The king is unwise, his associates are wicked, his chief councillor is a knave, and his minister, a scoundrel. Yet the people are many; why is not such misconduct resented?"

The Brahmans reply, "The manners of the people are equally depraved; they are valiant in oppression, skilful in falsehood, and persevering only in contempt for the pious."

Satyacharya asks, "How are the scribes?"

The Brahmans answer, "They collect the revenues by any expedient, and vigilantly inflict penalties on the wise. The Brahmans are not allowed to keep even the dust upon their bodies; the dust accumulated on their feet is claimed by the Kayeths. What can we say of this reign? The dumb alone can speak the truth, the deaf hear the law, the sons of the barren are well-behaved, the blind behold the observance of the scriptures. Our lands have been given to drunkards, and we are detained in prison for what our ancestors expended."

Satyacharya observes, "I have heard enough. Better fortunes attend you."

The general Samara Jambuka, the jackal of war, boasts that he can cleave a roll of butter with his falchion. He trembles from top to toe at the approach of a mosquito.

The king orders vice to be proclaimed virtue by beat of drum. All the Brahmans are perpetually banished.

PRACHANDA PANDAVA

or

THE OFFENDED SONS OF PANDU

or

BALA BHARATA

Draupadi is married to the five sons of Pandu, in compliance with the command of their mother. Yudhishthira, the eldest son of Pandu, loses every thing including Draupadi at chess-play with Duryodhana, the eldest of the Kauravas. Draupadi is now dragged by the hair, almost naked, into the public assembly, an insult in revenge for which ferocious Bhima vows to slay Duhsasana, the insulter, and drink his blood, and ultimately fulfils his vow. The Pandava princes then depart to the forest.

PROBODHA CHANDRODAYA

or

"RISE OF THE MOON OF (TRUE) KNOWLEDGE"

Religion and the noble king Reason, accompanied by all the Virtues namely Faith, Volition, Opinion, Imagination, Contemplation, Devotion, Quietude, Friendship and others, are banished, from Benares, by the evil king Error who reigns at Benares, surrounded by his faithful adherents, the Follies and Vices namely Self-conceit, Hypocrisy, Love, Passion, Anger, Avarice and others. There is, however, a prophecy that Reason will some day be reunited with Revelation; the fruit of the union will be True Knowledge, that will destroy the reign of Error.

The struggle for this union and its consummation are followed by the final triumph of the good party.

NAGANANDA

or

JOY OF THE SERPENTS

Jimutavahana, a prince of the Vidyadharas, is a Buddhist. He marries Malayavati, daughter of the king of the Siddhas, a votary of the goddess Gauri, the wife of the great god Siva. When he comes to know that Garuda, the bird celebrated in mythology, is used to eat up one snake each day, he makes up his mind to offer himself to the bird as a victim, and eventually succeeds in converting Garuda to the principle of *Ahimsa* or abstention from slaughter; but he himself is on the point of succumbing to the wounds he has received, when, through the timely intervention of the goddess Gouri, he recovers.

DUTANGADA

or

THE MISSION OF ANGADA

Angada, the son of Bali, is sent by Rama to Ravana to demand Sita. He executes his mission in a most clever and courageous manner. He then departs from Lanka. Ravana now goes forth to battle and is slain by Rama. The divine hero then enters the city of Lanka in triumph.

PRADYUMNA VIJAYA

A pair of geese, the *Hansa* and *Hansi* inspire Prabhavati, the daughter of Vajranabha, and Pradyumna, the son of Krishna with a mutual passion before they have beheld each other. By their contrivance, secret nuptials are brought about.

The sage Nareda communicates the stolen interviews of the lovers to the father of the damsel, to whose vengeance Pradyumna is about to fall a victim, when Krishna and Baladeva with their followers come to the rescue. A combat ensues in which Vajranabha is defeated and slain. The engagement is seen by two Gandherbas from their chariots in the air.

VIDAGDHA MADHAVA

The loves of Krishna and Radha are intense. The two lovers often engage in jealous squabbles.

Chandravali, a nymph of Vrindavan, is enamoured of Krishna and thus excites the jealousy of Radha.

The Paurnamasi, the personified day of the full moon, interests herself in the union of Krishna and Radha.

DHANANYAYA VIJAYA

The cattle of king Virat are carried off by Karna and the Kuru princes. Aryuna recovers them after a great battle. The different chiefs appear, threaten one another and praise themselves.

Indra and some of his attendants contemplate the fight from the clouds.

HASYARNAVA

The king Anasayindhu, in his progress through his city, re-grets to find everything subverted: that Chandals, not Brahmans, make shoes; that wives are chaste and husbands constant; and that respect is paid to the respectable, not to the vile; and that Vyadhisindhu, the doctor, cures the cholic by applying a heated needle to the palate, and perforates the pupils of the eyes in order to restore vision.

Sadhhinsaka, the chief of police, reports with great satisfac-tion that the city is completely in the hands of thieves; the Com-mander-in-chief Ranajambuka, after putting on his armour, valiantly cuts a leech in two. Mahayatrika, the astrologer, in an-swer to a question of the time to take a journey, indicates hours and positions which proclaim approaching death.

A dispute ensues between Viswabhanda, a Saiva mendicant, and Kalahankura, his disciple, which they refer to the decision of Mahanindaka, another Brahman, who asserts that he composed the *vedas* and visited *Swerga*, where he treated Vrihaspati and Brahma with contempt and gave Siva a drubbing.

CHITRA YAJNA

Daksha, the father of Sati or Bhavani and father-in-law of the great god Siva, institutes a great sacrifice.

The gods and sages assemble on the occasion, Daksha accords them a cordial reception. He bows down to the feet of the gods, and puts the dust from under them upon his head. He then proceeds to the place of sacrifice, reading or reciting the usual formulæ. He orders the attendants to distribute rice to the Brahmans, for the purpose of invoking their benedictions. They receive the rice, scatter it and pronounce the *Swasti Vachana*, or benedictory text. He offers oblation to fire.

Dadhichi now comes to the sacrifice, when a dispute ensues between him and the sacrificer, upon the impropriety of omitting to invite Siva; and the dispute becoming rather hot, Daksha orders his guest to be turned out. The gods partake of Dadhichi's indignation at the disrespectful mention of Siva, and rise to depart. Daksha orders his servants to guard the door and prevent their going forth: the gods, however, force their way.

The sages then also withdraw, on which Daksha goes out, exclaiming, "I will give double presents to those who remain." Nareda goes to Kailas with the news. He enters playing the *Vina* and singing hymns in honour of the great god. Nareda's communication to Siva and Bhavani is very brief.

Siva asks, "Now, Nareda, whence come you?" Nareda replies, "Your godship is omniscient, you know all that has happened, but have asked me through a wish to hear it from my lips. We were all invited to Daksha's sacrifice. Dadhichi, finding that you were not invited, took Daksha to task pretty sharply, and walked off, upon which I come to pay you my respects." Having said this and prostrated himself on the ground, the sage, with his lute hanging upon his neck, departed.

Sati now asks leave to go and see her father.

Siva replies, "It is quite contrary to etiquette, to go without an invitation." She answers, "I need not stand on ceremony with my father."

Siva observes, "How! would you impose upon me with falsehoods? Daksha is not your father, nor is his wife your mother, you are the father of all things, the mother of the universe. Those versed in the *Vedas* declare you male and female too."

In the end, she is allowed to follow her own inclinations.

She comes to her father, and vainly endeavours to impress

him with respect for her husband. She quits him to throw herself into the sacrificial fire.

Nareda then appears and tells Daksha to prepare for the consequences of his folly. Virabhadra, Siva's attendant, then enters and plays some antics. Shaking the earth with his tread, and filling space with his extended arms, he rolls his eyes in wrath. Some of the gods he casts on the ground and tramples on them; he knocks out the teeth of some with his fists, plucks out the beards of some, and cuts off the ears, arms, and noses of others; he smites some, and he tosses others into the sacrificial fire. He decapitates the cause of his master's indignation, the haughty Daksha.

MRIGANKALEKHA

Mrigankalekha is the daughter of the king of Kamarupa or Assam: she is beheld by Karpuratilaka, the king of Kalinga, whilst hunting, and the parties are mutually enamoured.

The obstacle to their union is the love of Sankhapala, a demon, to oppose whose supernatural powers, Ratnachura, the minister of the king of Kalinga, who alone is aware of the circumstance, invites to the palace a benevolent magician, Siddhayogini, and Mrigankalekha is also lodged in the palace as the friend of the queen Vilasavati.

Notwithstanding these precautions, she is carried off by Sankhapala to the temple of Kali, which is surrounded by goblins. During the Raja's peregrinations in his love-frenzy, he passes disconsolate through a wood in which he inquires of different animals if they have seen his mistress.

He now comes to the temple, rescues her, and kills Sankhapala. He is then united to Mrigankalekha in the presence of her father and brother, and with the consent of the queen. Before the conclusion of the marriage rite, he kills also the brother of Sankhapala, who comes to revenge him in the form of a wild elephant.

The marriage is thus effected through the secret contrivance of the minister, because the lady's husband is to become the master of the world.

MUDRARAKSHASA

or

RAKSHASA (THE MINISTER) WITH THE SIGNET

or

RAKSHASA AND THE SIGNET-RING

or

RAKSHASA KNOWN BY THE SIGNET-RING

The city of Pataliputra or Palibothra, the capital of the Nandas, was situated not far from the confluence of the Ganges and the Sone; and was on the southern side of the rivers. Nanda, the last king of the Nanda line, had for his minister the able and experienced Rakshasa. Chandragupta also called Vrishala and Maurya is identical with Sandrakottus represented by the Greek writers as the most powerful Raja in India at the time of Alexander the Great's death. He was a sovereign of dignity and strength of character and had a high respect for his minister Chanakya, the Indian Macchiavelli, who was a crafty, clearheaded, self-confident, intriguing and hard politician, with the ultimate end of his ambition thoroughly well-determined and directing all his clearheadedness and intrigue to the accomplishment of that end. This minister, also called Vishnugupta, is famous as a writer on *Nity* or "rules of government and polity", and the reputed author of numerous moral and political precepts commonly current in India. Nanda is slain by the contrivances of this wily Brahman, who thus assists Chandragupta to the throne, and becomes his minister. Rakshasa refuses to recognise the usurper and endeavours to be avenged on him for the ruin of his late master.

After the assassination of Nanda, Servarthasiddhi is placed on the throne by Rakshasa but he retires to a life of devotion. Saileswara or Parvataka or Parvateswara, the king of the Mountains, at first the ally of Chandragupta, afterwards befriended his opponents and is therefore slain privily by Chanakya. Vairodhaka, the brother of Parvataka, is killed by Rakshasa's emissaries by mistake for Chandragupta.

Malayaketu, the son of Parvataka, is a prince whose confidence and distrust are alike misplaced, who is thoughtless, suspicious, wanting in dignity, and almost child-like, not to say childish. He leads an army against Chandragupta but without success. He is so rash and inconsiderate as to resolve most hastily to undertake war against five kings at a time.

Rakshasa is a brave soldier but a blundering and somewhat soft-natured politician, whose faithfulnesss to his original master Nanda prompts him to wreak vengeance on Chandragupta and Chanakya. He has ultimately to abandon in despair his self-imposed task, the great aim of his life, being foiled by the arts of his adversary Chanakya. The proximate motive of the abandonment, however, is the duty of repaying favours received by him when he was engaged in his attempts at vengeance. He accidentally acquires a ring.

Chanakya, whose ability and diplomatic skill are of a high order, lays out various plottings and machinations to make Chandragupta the paramount sovereign in India, by winning over the noble Rakshasa to his master's cause. He tries successfully to effect a reconciliation between his protegé, and Rakshasa. With this view Rakshasa is rendered by the contrivances of Chanakya an object of suspicion to the prince Malyaketu with whom he has taken refuge and is consequently dismissed by him.

In this deserted condition he learns the imminent danger of a dear friend Chandandasa whom Chanakya is about to put to death, and in order to effect his liberation surrenders himself to his enemies.

They offer him, contrary to his expectations, the rank and power of Prime Minister, and the parties are finally friends.

The Nanda dynasty thus comes to an end and Chandragupta becomes the founder of the Maurya dynasty.

A curious scene in the last Act may be noticed here. A Chandala or executioner leads a criminal to the place of execution. The latter bears a stake (*Sula*) on his shoulder, and is followed by his wife and son who use no expressions suggestive of tenderness but only of sacrifice—a stern sense of duty. At the impending execution of her husband, she neither faints nor becomes disconsolate but simply weeps and talks of her duty.

The executioner calls out—"Make way, make way, good people! let every one who wishes to preserve his life, his property, or his family, avoid transgressing against the king as he would, poison." This criminal is Chandan Das who is put into chains with a view to force his friend Rakshsa to yield. He gives up his life and property for the sake of his friend Rakshasa. This conduct is described as casting into the shade the noble acts of even the Buddhas.

VIDDHA SALABHANJIKA

or

THE CARVED STATUE

Vidyadhar Malla, the chief of the Karachuli race, a Rajput tribe, was the king of Triling and Kalinga. Bhagurayana was his minister. Charayana was his Vidushaka or confidential attendant. Chandraverma, the king of Lata, was the maternal uncle-in-law of Vidyadhar Malla. He had no son. To satisfy his desire for a son, he dressed his only daughter Mrigankavali as a son to pass her off as such. People knew that the child was a son.

Bhagurayana had heard from the sages that "whosoever shall wed the daughter of Chandravarma shall become the paramount sovereign." So he told Chandravarma, "My king desires to see your son." Upon this Chandravarma sent his child to the queen of Vidyadhara Malla to be taken care of by her. Thus the minister contrived to bring Mrigankavali to the palace of his king.

One day, while the king is asleep, Mrigankavali puts a necklace on the neck of the king, being induced by a maid-servant who had instructions to do so by the minister. The king takes this as a wonderful dream. The vision of a beautiful maid agitates his mind. The king thus relates to Bidushaka the story of his fancied vision, "for the burden of the heart is lightened by sharing it with a faithful friend."

"A glorious halo appeared before me in my dream, bright as the moon's resplendent disk; within the orb a beauteous maiden moved as gently radiant as the lunar rays in autumn skies. Advancing near me, she inclined her head in reverence, and, as if pouring ambrosia into my ears, pronounced in softest tones, 'Glory to the deity of love!' Then sighing, she took up this string of costly pearls and placed it on my neck. This awoke me, I started up and saw my vision realised. I caught the nymph by her scarf, but she hastily extricated herself from my hands and fled, leaving me this necklace alone the evidence of her presence."

Bidushaka asks his Majesty, "Was not the queen with you when you dreamt? What did she do?"

The king replies, "The queen got angry and left me." Bidushaka remarks, "Why could not you assuage her anger?"

The king answers, "I was absorbed in the maid of my vision."

The Vidushaka, however, treats the whole as a dream, and

reproaches the king for his fickleness, as he had just before fallen in love with Kuvalayamala, the princess of Kuntala, and recommends him to be content with the queen, as "a partridge in the hand is better than a pea-hen in the forest."

The prince and the Vidushaka then go into the garden by the back-door, where, over the edge of a terrace, they see some of the fair tenants of the inner apartments amusing themselves with swinging. Amongst them the king recognises the countenance he has seen in his dream, but the party disappear on the advance of the king and his friend.

The king then enters a pleasure-house or pavilion called the *kelikailas* or mountain of sport built for him by the minister.

It is a beautiful palace built of crystal, and decorated with statues and paintings. One of the paintings is thus described:

"There is your Majesty at *pasa* (dice) with the queen: behind you stands one damsel with the betel box, whilst another is waving the *chownri* over your head: the dwarf is playing with the monkey, and the parrot abusing the Vidushaka." The chamber also contains the portrait of Mrigankavali, the damsel whom the prince has really seen in his supposed dream. There is also a statue of her, whence the drama is named *Viddha Salabhanjika*, meaning a curved statue or effigy.

The king discovers the statue. He thinks, "Who will carve on the wall the person I dreamed of? No one was present when I dreamt. Has anyone carved the statue out of his fancy? A real person may exist in this world or how can an exact figure come here?"

He now verily believes the dream to be a reality. He then puts the necklace of his dream on the neck of the carved statue.

Finally the lady is herself beheld through the transparent wall of the pavilion, but runs away on being observed. The king becomes enamoured of her. He and his friend follow her but in vain. The bards proclaim it at noon, and the two friends repair to the queen's apartments to perform the midday ceremonies.

Kuvalayamala, the object of the king's passion before encountering his new flame, is the daughter of Chandramahasena, the king of Kuntala. She has been sent to Vidyadhara Malla's queen, as the betrothed bride of the supposed son of Chandraverma, who is the queen's maternal uncle. Mekhala, the queen's foster-sister, practises a frolic on Charayana. He is promised a new bride by the queen, and the ceremony is about to take place when the spouse proves to be a "lubberly boy"; he is highly indignant at the trick, and goes off threatening vengeance.

The king having followed and pacified his companion, they go off into the garden, where they see the damsel Mrigankavali playing with ball: she still however flies their advance. Presently they overhear a conversation between her and one of her companions, from which it appears, that notwithstanding her shyness she is equally enamoured of the king.

Her dress is the contrivance of the minister, at whose instigation, Mrigankavali is persuaded by Sulakshana to believe that she is to behold the present deity of love, and is introduced by a sliding door into the king's chamber. The consequence of the interview is to render Mrigankavali passionately enamoured of the king.

One day, the queen, in order to deceive Charayana, manages to celebrate a marriage between him and a son of a maid-servant veiled as a female. The trick is discovered. He is highly indignant.

He now retaliates with the help of the king. He induces Sulakshana, one of the female attendants of the queen, to ascend a *Bakula* tree and thence send a message in a nasal tone, as if from the sky, to Mekhala, the foster-sister and chief attendant of the queen.

"Thou shalt die at this spot on the full moon day of *Baisakh*." After many entreaties, the heavenly voice prescribes a relief, "Thou art safe if thou canst pass through the legs of a Brahmin skilled in music and gratified with a fee." Charayana, just the kind of Brahmin required, arrives at this juncture. The king and the queen are present. Mekhala and the queen, both overcome with concern, entreat Charayana to be the Brahmin that shall preserve the life of the former. He consents. As Mekhala tries to pass between his legs, he mounts on her back and says, "you are now caught in your turn. You deceived me once. Now marry me." He triumphs in the humiliation he has inflicted on her. The queen now perceives the intrigue of the king, is in her turn incensed, goes off in a pet and resolves to take revenge.

Chandamahasen, the king of Kuntala as a defeated prince now resides with his daughter Kubalayamala under the protection of the victorious king. The king sees her one day as she rises after bathing in the Narbadda. He becomes enamoured of her and wishes to marry her. The queen gets scent of the matter. To prevent the curse of co-wifeship, the queen now resolves to get her husband married to the son of her maternal uncle so that he may be ashamed into abandoning his polygamous tendency.

The king and the Vidushaka seek the garden, where it is now moon-light. Mrigankavali and her friend Vilakshana also come thither, and the lovers meet: this interview is broken off by a cry that the queen is coming, and they all separate abruptly.

At dawn, Charayana's wife is asleep. In her sleep, however, she is very communicative, and repeats a supposed dialogue between the queen and the Raja, in which the former urges the latter to marry Mrigankavali, the sister of the supposed Mrigankavarma, come on a visit, it is pretended, to her brother—this being a plot of the queen's to cheat the king into a sham marriage, by espousing him to one she believes to be a boy.

The Vidushaka suspects the trick, however, and wakes his wife, who rises and goes to the queen. The Vidushaka joins his master. The king, who is already the husband of the princesses of Magadha, Malava, Panchala, Avanti, Jalandhara and Kerala, is wedded to Mrigankavali. As soon as the ceremony is gone through, a messenger from the court of Chandraverma arrives to announce:—

"O queen! His Majesty Chandravarma wishes it to be known that Mrigankavarma is not his son but his daughter. In the absence of a son he dressed her as such to satisfy his desire for a son. Now that a son has been born to him, it is not necessary to keep up the pretence. The king requests you to settle a suitable marriage for her. The sages have prophesied paramount sovereignty for her husband."

The queen becomes stunned and soliloquises:—

"What is play to me, Providence ordains to be a stern fact. Man proposes, God disposes." She now finds that she has taken herself in, and given herself another rival wife. As the matter is past remedy, however, she assents with a good grace. The minister is glad that his aims are fulfilled. All are happy, Why should Kuvalayamala alone be sorry? The queen therefore allows her lord to marry Kuvalyamala.

To crown the king's happiness, a messenger, sent by the General of His Majesty's forces, now arrives from the camp with the news that the allied armies of Kernata, Simhala, Pandya, Murala, Andhra, and Konkana have been defeated, and Virapala, king of Kuntala, the ally of Vidyadhara Malla, reseated on a throne, from which his kinsman, supported by those troops, had formerly expelled him. The authority of Vidyadhara Malla as paramount sovereign is now declared to extend from the mouths of the Ganges to the sea, and from the Narbada to the Tamraperni in the Deccan.

RATNAVALI

or

THE NECKLACE

A holy seer announces to Yaugandharayana, the chief minister of Vatsa, the king of Kausambi, that whoever shall wed
Ratnavali, the fair daughter of Vikramabahu, the king of *Sinhala*
or Ceylon and maternal uncle of Vasavadatta, the queen of Vatsa,
should become the emperor of the world. The faithful minister,
desirous of securing paramount sovereignty for his master, sends,
without his knowledge and consent, an envoy to the court of
Vikramabahu to negotiate the match. Vikramabahu declines to
inflict the curse of co-wifeship upon his daughter and niece. The
disappointed envoy returns home.

The premier is sorry, but does not lose hope. After much
deliberation, he hits upon an ingenious device. He proclaims in
Ceylon by agents that queen Vasavadatta is dead, being burnt by
chance and that the king, though much grieved, has at last consented, at the request of friends and relatives, to marry again. The
intelligence reaches the ears of Vikramabahu who believes it.

The premier now sends Babhravya as envoy to the Court of
Ceylon to reopen the question of Ratnavali's marriage with Vatsa.
Vikramabahu, after consulting his queen, consents to the proposal. He has Ratnavali decked in all ornaments including a
single-stringed necklace round her neck and sends her away on
board a ship, in company with his own ambassador Vasubhuti
and Babhravya. He waits on the shore till the ship is out of sight
and then returns home sorry at parting with his daughter.

A terrible tempest wrecks the ship. A merchant of Kausambi
finds Ratnavali floating in mid-sea, saves her life and brings her to
the minister who thanks him heartily for the favour and offers a
reward. The merchant thus expresses his unwillingness to accept
it, "Sir, under the rule of our gracious king, the weak do not fear
the strong; the rich cannot oppress the poor; the word 'robber'
has become obsolete; the sick and the orphans are being treated
by the best of physicians and are free from any want of food and
clothing; children are being properly educated; drought is never
heard of; the highways are wide, clean, and well-guarded; com-
munications are safe. If any loyal subject can be of any service to
such a king, he does only his bare duty and should not accept any
reward." He at last accepts the reward at the repeated requests of

the minister and goes home.

Then the minister interviews the queen, conceals the real facts and addresses her thus:—

"May it please your Majesty. I have received this girl from a merchant who told me that he had rescued her in the sea, but could not say anything more about her and her whereabouts. From her appearance she seems to be a respectable lady. I beseech your Majesty to take care of her." The queen takes the girl as one of her attendants—the girl who is destined to make her husband the lord of the world! The queen names her Sagarika or the Ocean Maid. The princess, who has been attended by hundreds of maid-servants, is now reduced, by a strange irony of fate, to the position of a maid-servant herself!

The Chamberlain Babhravya and Vasubhuti by some means reach the shore and are on their way to *Kausambi*.

Vatsa comes forth to behold from the terrace of his palace the frolic merriment with which his subjects celebrate the festival of *Kamadeva*, the god of love. Wearied of tales of war, and seeking most his reputation in his people's hearts, he issues forth attended by his confidential companion Vasantaka, like the flower-armed deity himself, descended to take a part in the happiness of his wor-shippers. The king observes:—

"I scarcely can express the content I now enjoy. My kingdom is rid of every foe; the burden of my government reposes on able shoulders; the seasons are favourable; and my subjects, pros-perous and happy. In Vasavadatta, the daughter of Pradyota, I have a wife whom I adore, and in Vasantaka, a friend in whom I can confide. Attended by such a friend, at such a season, and so disposed I might fancy myself the deity of desire, and this vernal celebration held in honour of myself. Kausambi outvies the resi-dence of the god of wealth. Her numerous sons are clad in cloth of gold, decked with glittering ornaments and tossing their heads proudly with splendid crests.

Vasantaka says:—

"Observe the general joy. As if intoxicated with delight, the people dance along the streets, sporting merrily with each other's persons and mutually scattering the yellow-tinted fluid. On every side, the music of the drum and the buzz of frolic crowds fill all the air. The very atmosphere is of a yellow hue, with clouds of flowery fragrance."

At the request of the queen, conveyed through her attendants, the king proceeds with his friend to join her in offering homage to the image of the flower-armed deity, which stands at the foot of the red *Asoka* tree. The queen enters the garden accompanied by Kanchanmala, her principal attendant, Sagarika and other damsels. Noticing Sagarika, the queen thinks, "What carelessness! an object I have hitherto so cautiously concealed, thus heedlessly exposed! I must remove her hence before the arrival of the king." She says, "How now, Sagarika, what makes you here? where is my favourite starling, that I left to your charge, and whom it seems you have quitted for this ceremony? Return to your place." Sagarika withdraws to a short distance and thinks, "the bird is safe with my friend Susangata. I should like to witness the ceremony. I wonder if *Annaga* is worshipped here as in my father's mansion! I will keep myself concealed amongst the shrubs and watch them, and for my own presentation to the deity I will go, cull a few of these flowers." The king now joins the queen. Kanchanmala delivers the accustomed gifts of sandal, saffron, and flowers to the queen, who offers them to the image. The king thus eulogises the beauty of the queen, "Whilst thus employed, my love, you resemble a graceful creeper turning round a coral tree: your robes of the orange dye, your person fresh from the bath. As rests your hand upon the stem of the *Asoka*, it seems to put forth a new and lovelier shoot. The unembodied god to-day will regret his disencumbered essence, and sigh to be material, that he might enjoy the touch of that soft hand."

The worship of the divinity concluded, the queen worships the king. Sagarika views the scene, mistakes the king for the god and observes, "What do I see? Can this be true? Does then the deity, whose effigy only we adore in the dwelling of my father, here condescend to accept in person the homage of his votaries? I, too, though thus remote, present my humble offering."

She throws down the flowers and continues:—"Glory to the flower-armed god: may thy auspicious sight both now and hereafter prove not to have been vouchsafed to me in vain!"

She bows down, then rising looks again, and observes:—

"The sight, though oft repeated, never wearies. I must tear myself from this, lest some one should discover me." She then withdraws a little, hears a bard sing a ballad in praise of the king, perceives her mistake and asks herself, "Is this Udayana, to whom my father destined me a bride?" She becomes enamoured of the king. The king and the queen now rise to return to the palace.

Sagarika thinks, "They come! I must fly hence. Ah me, unhappy! no longer to behold him, whom I could gaze upon for ever."

The king addresses his queen thus:—"Come, love, thou puttest the night to shame. The beauty of the moon is eclipsed by the loveliness of thy countenance, and the lotus sinks humbled into shade; the sweet songs of thy attendant damsels discredit the murmurs of the bees, and mortified they hasten to hide their disgrace within the flowery blossom." The king and the queen return to the palace.

Sagarika enters a plantain bower with a brush and pallet in order to paint a picture and soliloquises thus: "Be still, my foolish heart, nor idly throb for one so high above thy hopes. Why thus anxious to behold that form, one only view of which has inspired such painful agitation? Ungrateful, too, as weak, to fly the breast that has been familiar to thee through life, and seek another, and as yet but once beheld, asylum. Alas! Why do I blame thee! the terror of *Ananga's* shaft has rendered thee a fugitive;—let me implore his pity. Lord of the flowery bow, victor of demons and of gods! dost thou not blush to waste thy might upon a weak defenceless maiden, or art thou truly without form and sense? Ah me, I fear my death impends, and this the fatal cause." She looks at the picture and goes on, "No one approaches; I will try and finish the likeness I am here attempting to portray. My heart beats high, my hand trembles, yet I must try, and whilst occasion favours me, attempt to complete these lineaments, as the only means to retain them in my sight." She draws the picture, raising her head beholds her friend Susangata with a *Sarika* or talking bird in a cage, and hides the picture. Susangata sits down, puts her hand upon the picture and asks, "who is this you have delineated?"

Sagarika answers, "The deity of the festival, *Ananga*." Susangata observes, "It is cleverly done, but there wants a figure to complete it. Let me have it, and I will give the god his bride." She takes the paper and draws the likeness of Sagarika. Sagarika expresses anger. Her friend remarks, "Do not be offended without cause. I have given your *Kamadeva* my *Rati*, that is all. But come, away with disguise, and confess the truth." Seeing that her friend has discovered her secret, Sagarika is overcome with shame and entreats her to promise that no body else shall be made acquainted with her weakness. Her friend replies, "why should you be ashamed? Attachment to exalted worth becomes your native excellence. But be assured I will not betray you; it is more likely this prattling bird will repeat our conversation." The friend brings some leaves and fibres of the lotus, and binds the former with the latter upon Sagarika's bosom. She exclaims, "Enough, enough, my friend, take away these leaves and fibres,—it is vain to offer relief. I have fixed my heart where I dare not raise my hopes. I am overcome with shame—I am enslaved by passion—my love is without return—death, my only refuge." She faints and recovers after a short while. A noise behind proclaims that a monkey has escaped from the stable, and, rattling the ends of his broken chain of gold, he clatters along. Afraid of the advent of the monkey, they both rush to hide in the shade of a *tamala* grove, leaving the drawing behind. The ape breaks the cage to get at the curds and rice and lets the *Sarika* fly.

Vasantaka now notices that the jasmine has been covered with countless buds, as if smiling disdainfully upon the queen's favourite *Madhavi*. He is surprised at the most marvellous power of the venerable Sri-Khanda-Dasa, a great sage come to court from *Sri-Parvata*, by whose simple will the strange event has happened. He thinks of going to the king to inform his Majesty when the king appears. He congratulates his Majesty, on his propitious fortune. The king observes, "Inconceivable is the virtue of drugs, and charms, and gems. Lead the way, and let these eyes this day obtain by the sight the fruit of their formation."

Vasantaka advances, stops to listen and turns back in alarm for he fancies a goblin in yonder *Bakula* tree. The goblin turns out a starling. The courtier remarks, "she says, give the Brahman something to eat." The king observes, "something to eat is ever the burden of the glutton's song. Come, say truly, what does she utter." The friend listens and repeats, "Who is this you have delineated? Do not be offended without cause; I have given your *Kamadeva* my *Rati*. Why should you be ashamed? Attachment to exalted worth becomes your native excellence. Take away these lotus leaves and fibres—it is in vain you strive to offer me relief. I have fixed my heart where I dare not raise my hopes;—I am overcome with shame and despair, and death is my only refuge." The king interprets thus:—"Oh, I suppose some female has been drawing her lover's portrait, and passing it off on her companion as the picture of the god of love: her friend has found her out; and ingeniously exposed her evasion, by delineating her in the character of *Kama-deva's* bride. The lady that is pictured is very handsome. Some young female may be supposed to have spoken, indifferent to life, because uncertain of her affection being returned. The delicate maid entrusts her companion with the sorrows of her breast: the tattling parrot or imitative starling repeats her words, and they find an hospitable welcome in the ears of the fortunate. The companion, laughing loudly, observes, "You may as well drop these evasive interpretations; why not say at once, 'the damsel doubts my returning her passion.' Who but yourself could have been delineated as the god of the flowery bow?"

The friend claps his hands and laughs. His obstreperous mirth frightens the bird away. She perches on the plantain bower. They follow her there. Vasantaka finds a picture and shows it to the king, who gives him a golden bracelet. Looking at it, the king dwells upon the beauties of the damsel.

Susangata and Sagarika hide themselves behind the plantain trees and overhear the conversation between the king and his companion. Susangata remarks, "You are in luck, girl; your lover is dwelling upon your praises. The bird, as I told you, has repeated our conversation." Sagarika thinks to herself, "What will he reply? I hang between life and death." The king remarks farther to his companion, "My sight insatiate rests upon her graceful limbs and slender waist. I cannot deny that she has flatteringly delineated my likeness, nor doubt her sentiments—for observe the traces of the tear that has fallen upon her work, like the moist dew that starts from every pore of my frame." Sagarika says to herself, "Heart, be of good cheer! your passion is directed to a corresponding object." Susangata now comes forward, so as to be seen by Vasantaka. At this the king, on the advice of his companion, covers the picture with his mantle. Susangata says, "I am acquainted with the secret of the picture and some other matters of which I shall apprise her Majesty." The king takes off his bracelet and other ornaments and offers them to her with the object of bribing her to be silent. She replies, "Your Majesty is bountiful. You need not fear me. I was but in jest, and do not want these jewels. The truth is, my dear friend, Sagarika is very angry with me for drawing her picture, and I shall be much obliged to your Majesty to intercede for me and appease her resentment." The king springs up and exclaims, "Where is she? Lead me to her."

Then all advance to Sagarika. She thinks, "He is here—I tremble at his sight. I can neither stand nor move—what shall I do?" Vasantaka, seeing her, exclaims, "A most surprising damsel, truly; such another is not to be found in this world. I am confident that when she was created, *Brahma* was astonished at his own performance." The king is struck with her and observes, "such are my impressions. The four mouths of *Brahma* must at once have exclaimed in concert, bravo, bravo! when the deity beheld these eyes more beauteous than the leaves of his own lotus; and his head must have shaken with wonder, as he contemplated her loveliness, the ornament of all the world." Sagarika prepares to go away when the king addresses her thus, "You turn your eyes upon your friend in anger, lovely maid; yet such is their native tenderness that they cannot assume a harsh expression. Look thus, but do not leave us, for your departure hence will alone give me pain." Susangata now advises the king to take Sagarika by the hand and pacify her. The king approves the advice and acts up to it. Vasantaka congratulates the king on his unprecedented fortune.

The king replies, "You say rightly—she is the very deity Lakshmi herself. Her hand is the new shoot of the *Parijata* tree, else whence distil these dewdrops of ambrosia?" Susangata remarks, "It is not possible, my dear friend, you can remain inexorable whilst honoured thus with his Majesty's hand."

Sagarika frowns on her friend and asks her to forbear. At this time, Vasantaka, in testiness of temper, raises a false alarm by proclaiming that the queen is approaching. The king lets go Sagarika's hand in alarm. Sagarika and her companion go off hastily behind the *tamala* tree.

After a short time, the queen approaches the king. By order of the king, Vasantaka hides the picture quickly under his arm. The king proposes to visit, in the company of the queen, the Jasmine budded. The queen declines. Vasantaka takes it as an acknowledgment of defeat on her part and cries out Huzza! He waves his hand and dances; the picture falls. Kanchanmala, an attendant of the queen, picks up the picture and shows it to her mistress. The queen, whose jealousy is excited by the discovery of the picture, demands an explanation from the king. Vasantaka volunteers to offer the explanation thus:—"I was observing, madam, that it would be very difficult to hit my friend's likeness, on which his Majesty was pleased to give me this specimen of his skill." The king confirms the explanation. The queen observes, "And the female standing near you—I suppose this is a specimen of Vasantaka's skill." The king replies, "What should you suspect? That is a mere fancy portrait, the original was never seen before." Vasantaka supports the king thus, "I will swear to this, by my Brahmanical thread, that the original was never seen before by either of us." Not satisfied with the explanation, the queen remarks, "My lord, excuse me. Looking at the picture has given me a slight headache. I leave you to your amusements."

The king observes, "What can I say to you, dearest? I really am at a loss. If I ask you to forgive me, that is unnecessary, if you are not offended; and how can I promise to do so no more, when I have committed no fault, although you will not believe my assertions?" The queen, detaching herself gently and with politeness, takes leave and goes away with her attendant. Vasantaka remarks, "Your Majesty has had a lucky escape. The queen's anger has dispersed like summer clouds." The king observes. "Away, block-head, we have no occasion to rejoice; could you not discover the queen's anger through her unsuccessful attempts to disguise it? Her face was clouded with a passing frown. As she hung down her head, she looked on me with an affected smile. She gave utterance to no angry words, it is true, and the swelling eye glowed not with rage—but a starting tear was with difficulty repressed; and although she treated me with politeness, struggling indignation lurked in every gesture. We must endeavour to pacify her."

To insure the vigilance of Kanchanmala, the queen gives her some of her own clothes and ornaments. With these it is plotted to equip Sagarika as the queen. A stolen interview between the king and Sagarika, thus disguised, is arranged to take place at the *Madhava* bower about sunset. The queen gets scent of the matter and forestalls Sagarika by meeting the king at the appointed time and place. The king, mistaking her for Sagarika, thus speaks his honest self! "My beloved Sagarika, thy countenance is radiant as the moon, thy eyes are two lotus buds, thy hand is the full blown flower, and thy arms, its graceful filaments. Come thou, whose form is the shrine of ecstasy, come to my arms."

The queen throws off her veil and says:—"Believe me still Sagarika, my good lord; your heart is so fascinated by her, you fancy you behold Sagarika in everything." The king replies, "forgive me, dearest." The queen remarks, "Address not this to me, my lord—the epithet is another's property." The king falls at her feet. The queen observes, "Rise, my lord, rise! that wife must be unreasonable indeed, who, with such evidence of her lord's affection, can presume to be offended. Be happy, I take my leave." She now goes away.

Sagarika, dressed as the queen, goes some way to meet the king when she thinks of putting an end at once to her sufferings and her life and fastens the noose round her neck with the fibres of the *Madhavi*. The king, who is seeking for the queen in hopes to pacify her anger, discovers Sagarika on the way and mistakes her for the queen. He rushes to her and tears off the tendril. He soon discovers his mistake, embraces her and observes, "When the bosom of my queen swells with sighs, I express concern; when she is sullen, I soothe her; when her brows are bent, and her face is distorted with anger, I fall prostrate at her feet. These marks of respect are due to her exalted position; but the regard that springs from vehement affection, that is yours alone."

At this time, the queen, who has overheard the speech, comes forward and says, "I believe you, my lord, I believe you." The king explains his conduct thus:—"Why, then, you need not be offended. Cannot you perceive that I have been attracted hither, and misled by the resemblance of your dress and person? Be composed, I beg you." He falls at her feet. She observes, "Rise, rise, let not my exalted station put you to such unnecessary inconvenience."

Vasantaka takes up the noose, shows it to the queen and explains his conduct thus, "It is very true, madam, I assure you, that, deceived by the belief that you were attempting to destroy yourself, I brought my friend to this spot, to preserve, as I thought, your life." By order of the queen, Kanchanmala puts the noose over his neck, beats him and carries him off an unfortunate captive. The king thinks, "What an unlucky business this is! What is to be done? How shall I dissipate the rage that clouds the smiling countenance of the queen! How rescue Sagarika from the dread of her resentment, or liberate my friend Basantaka? I am quite bewildered with these events, and can no longer command my ideas. I will go in, and endeavour to pacify the queen." The queen regales Vasantaka with cakes from her own fair hands, presents him with a dress and restores him to liberty. Susangata prays him to accept a diamond necklace which Sagarika has left with her for presentation to him. He declines the offer. Looking at it attentively he wonders where she could have procured such a valuable necklace. They both go to the king who has gone from the queen's apartments to the crystal alcove and is lamenting thus:—"Deceitful vows, tender speeches, plausible excuses and prostrate supplications had less effect upon the queen's anger than her own teaks; like water upon the fire they quenched the blaze of her indignation. I am now only anxious for Sagarika. Her form, as delicate as the petal of the lotus, dissolving in the breath of inexperienced passion, has found a passage through the channels by which love penetrates, and is lodged deep in my heart. The friend to whom I could confide my secret sorrows is the prisoner of the queen." Vasantaka now informs the king that he has been restored to liberty. Asked about Sagarika he hangs down his head and declares that he cannot utter such unpleasant tidings. The king infers that Sagarika is no more and faints. The friend says, "my friend, revive—revive! I was about to tell you, the queen has sent her to Ougein—this I called unpleasant tidings, Susangata told me so,— and what is more, she gave me this necklace to bring to your Majesty." Vasantaka gives the king the necklace which he applies to his heart to alleviate his despair. By command, the courtier applies the ornament round the neck of the king. At this time, Vijayavarman, the nephew of Rumanwat the general of the state, arrives to announce:—"Glory to your Majesty! your Majesty's fortune is propitious in the triumphs of Rumanwat. By your Majesty's auspices the *Kosalas* are subdued. On receiving your Majesty's commands, my uncle soon collected a mighty army of foot, and horse, and elephants, and marching against the king of Kosala, surrounded him in a strong position in the Vindhya mountains. Impatient of the blockade, the *Kosala* monarch prepared his troops for an engagement. Issuing from the heights, the enemy's forces came down upon us in great numbers, and the points of the horizon were crowded with the array of mighty elephants, like another chain of mountains: they bore down our infantry beneath their ponderous masses: those who escaped the shock were transpierced by innumerable arrows and the enemy flattered himself he had for once disappointed our commander's hopes. Fires flashed from the blows of contending heroes, helmets and heads were cloven in twain—the broken armour and scattered weapons were carried away in torrents of blood, and the defiance of the king of *Kosala*, in the van of his army, was heard by our warriors; when our chief alone confronted him, and slew the monarch on his furious elephant with countless shafts. All honour to our gallant foe, the king of *Kosala*; for glorious is the warrior's death when his enemies applaud his prowess. Rumanwat then appointed my elder brother, Sanjayavarman, to govern the country of *Kosala*, and making slow marches in consequence of the number of his wounded, returned to the capital. He is now arrived." The king applauds his general and commands the distribution of the treasures of his favour.

Samvarasiddhi, a magician from Ougein, now interviews the king. The magician, waving a bunch of peacock's feathers, observes, "Reverence to Indra, who lends our art his name. What are your Majesty's commands? Would you see the moon brought down upon earth, a mountain in mid air, a fire in the ocean, or night at noon? I will produce them—Command. What need of many words? By the force of my master's spells, I will place before your eyes the person whom in your heart you are most anxious to behold."

The king not wishing to see the performance alone, summons the queen who arrives soon. The king leads her to a seat, sits beside her and commands the magician to display his power.

The magician waves his plumes and exhibits most wonderful scenes. *Brahma* appears throned upon the lotus; *Sankara* appears with the crescent moon, his glittering crest; *Hari*, the destroyer of the demon race, in whose four hands the bow, the sword, the mace and the shell are borne, is observable. *Indra*, the king of *Swarga*, is seen mounted on his stately elephant. Around them countless spirits dance merrily in mid air, sporting with the lovely nymphs of heaven, whose anklets ring responsive to the measure. The king and queen look up and rise from their seats. At this time, a female attendant appears to announce;—"So please your Majesty, the minister Yaugandharayana begs to inform you, that Vikrambahu, the king of Ceylon, has sent, along with your own messenger who returns, the councillor Vasubhuti; be pleased to receive him as the season is auspicious. The minister will also wait upon you as soon as he is at leisure." The queen observes, "Suspend this spectacle, my lord. Vasubhuti is a man of elevated rank; he is also of the family of my maternal uncle, and should not be suffered to wait; let us first see him." The king orders the suspension of the show, the magician retires promising to exhibit yet some sights.

Vasubhuti, after the customary exchange of courtesies, thus relates his story:—"In consequence of the prophesy of a seer, that whoever should wed Ratnavali, my master's daughter, should become the emperor in the world, your Majesty's minister solicited her for your bride; unwilling, however, to be instrumental in the uneasiness of Vasavadatta, the king of Simhala declined compliance with his suit. My master, understanding at last that the queen was deceased, consented to give his daughter to you. We were deputed to conduct her hither, when alas, our vessel was wrecked." The envoy, overpowered by sorrows, is unable to continue the story and weeps. The queen exclaims, "Alas, unhappy that I am! Loved sister Ratnavali, where art thou? Near me and reply."

The king consoles the queen thus:—

"The fate that causes, may remove our sorrows."

A cry is now heard from behind that the inner apartments are on fire. The king starts up wildly and exclaims, "Vasavadatta burnt to death! my queen, my love!"

The queen exclaims, "What extravagance is this—behold me at your side. But ah! help, help, my lord. I think not of myself but poor Sagarika. She is in bonds; my cruelty has kept her captive—and she will be lost without some aid—haste, haste and save her!" The king flies to her rescue, precipitates himself into the flames and takes her in his arms. He pauses—looks around—closes his eyes, and reopens them. The flames disappear. The palace stands unharmed. The king observes, "This must have been a dream, or is it magic?" Vasantaka replies, "The latter, no doubt; did not that conjuring son of a slave say, he had still something for your Majesty to see?"

The king says to the queen,

"Here, madam, is Sagarika rescued in obedience to your commands." The queen smiling replies, "I am sensible of your obedience, my lord." She now informs all present, "Yaugandharayana presented her to me, and told me she had been rescued from the sea: it was hence we designated her Sagarika or the ocean Maid." The likeness—the necklace—the recovery of the damsel from the sea—leave no doubt in the mind of Vasubhuti that this is the daughter of the king of Simhala, Ratnavali. Vasubhuti advances to her who looks at him. They recognize each other and both faint. After some time they recover. As Ratnavali goes to embrace the queen at her invitation, she stumbles. At the request of the queen who blushes for her cruelty, the king takes the chains off Ratnavali's feet. Yaugandharayana now explains his conduct thus, "It was formerly announced to us by a holy seer, that the husband of the princess of Simhala should become the emperor of the world. We therefore earnestly applied to her father to give her hand to our sovereign; but unwilling to be cause of uneasiness to the queen, the monarch of Simhala declined compliance with our request: we therefore raised a report that Vasavadatta had perished by a fire at Lavanaka, and Babhravya was despatched with the news to the court of Simhala. Vikrambahu then consented to our proposal and sent his daughter on board a ship accompanied by Vasubhuti and Babhravya. The ship was wrecked. The princess was rescued from the sea by a merchant who brought her to me. I placed her with the queen in a very unsuitable station as I expected you would see her in the inner apartments, and take pleasure in her sight. I had some concern in the appearance of the magician who had conjured up a vision of the gods and a conflagration, as no other means remained of restoring the damsel to your presence and creating an opportunity for Vasubhuti to see and recognise the princess." The queen now puts on Ratnavali her own jewels, then takes her by the hand and presents her to the king. Ratnavali bows to the queen who embraces her. The king observes, "My cares are all rewarded. Nothing more is necessary, Vikrambahu is my kinsman, Sagarika, the essence of the world, the source of universal victory, is mine, and Vasavadatta rejoices to obtain a sister. The *Kosalas* are subdued: what other object does the world present for which I could entertain a wish? This be alone my prayer; may Indra with seasonable showers render the earth bountiful of grain; may the presiding Brahmans secure the favour of the gods by acceptable sacrifices; may the association of the pious confer delight until the end of time, and may the appalling blasphemies of the profane be silenced for ever."

APPENDIX
THE VALUE OF DRAMA

The purposes for which an ancient language may be studied are its philology and its literature, or the arts and sciences, the notions and manners, the history and beliefs of the people by whom it was spoken. Particular branches may be preferably cultivated for the understanding of each of these subjects, but there is no one species which will be found to embrace so many purposes as the dramatic. The dialogue varies from simple to elaborate, from the conversation of ordinary life to the highest refinements of poetical taste. The illustrations are drawn from every known product of art, as well as every observable phenomenon of nature. The manners and feelings of the people are delineated, living and breathing before us, and history and religion furnish the most important and interesting topics to the bard. Wherever, therefore, there exists a dramatic literature, it must be pre-eminently entitled to the attention of the philosopher as well as the philologist, of the man of general literary tastes as well as the professional scholar.

THE ORIGIN OF DRAMA

Among the various sorts of literary composition the drama holds the most important position; for it is a picture of real life, and, as such, of national interest. It consists of two principal species, tragedy and comedy; the minor species are tragi-comedy, farce, burlesque and melo-drama. Both tragedy and comedy attained their perfection in Greece long before the Christian era. There it originated in the worship of Bacchus.

The English drama took its rise from the mysteries or sacred plays by the medium of which the clergy in the Middle Ages endeavoured to impart a knowledge of the Christian religion.

The Sanskrit drama is said to have been invented by the sage Bharata, who lived at a very remote period of Indian history and was the author of a system of music. The earliest references to the acted drama are to be found in the *Mahabhashya*, which mentions representations of the *Kansabadha* and the *Balibadha*, episodes in the history of Krishna. Indian tradition describes Bharat as having caused to be acted before the gods a play representing the *Svayam-vara* of Lakshmi.

Tradition further makes Krishna and his cowherdesses the

starting point of the *Sangita*, a representation consisting of a mixture of song, music, and dancing. The Gitagovinda is concerned with Krishna, and the modern *Yatras* generally represent scenes from the life of that deity.

From all this it seems likely that the Hindu drama was developed in connection with the cult of Vishnu-Krishna; and that the earliest acted representations were, therefore, like the mysteries of the Christian Middle Ages, a kind of religious plays, in which scenes from the legends of the gods were enacted mainly with the aid of songs and dances supplemented with prose dialogues improvised by the performers. These earliest forms of Hindu dramatic literature are represented by those hymns of the *Rig-Veda* which contain dialogues such as those of Sarama and the Panis, Yama and Yami, Pururava and Urvaci.

The words for actor (*nata*) and play (*nataka*) are derived from the verb *nat*, the Prakrit or vernacular form of the Sanskrit *nrit*, "to dance." Hence scholars are of opinion that the Sanskrit drama has developed out of dancing. The representations of dramas of early times were attended with dancing and gesticulation. There were rude performances without the contrivances of stage and scenic arrangements, dancing and music forming a considerable part. The addition of dialogue was the last step in the development, which was thus much the same in India and Greece. This primitive stage is represented by the Bengal *Yaêras* and the Gitagovinda. These form the transition to the fully developed Sanskrit play in which lyrics and dialogue are blended.

Sakuntala belongs to the mytho-pastoral class of Sanskrit plays; Probodhchandraudya, to the metaphysical. The Hindu theatre affords examples of the drama of domestic, as well as of heroic life; of original invention as well as of legendary tradition.

The Hindus did not borrow their dramatic compositions from foreigners. The nations of Europe possessed no dramatic literature before the fourteenth or fifteenth century, at which period the Hindu drama had passed into its decline. Mohammedan literature has ever been a stranger to theatrical writings, and the Mussalman conquerors of India could not have communicated what they never possessed. There is no record that theatrical entertainments were ever naturalised amongst the ancient Persians, Arabs, or Egyptians. With the exception of a few features in common with the Greek and the Chinese dramas, which could not fail to occur independently, the Hindu dramas present characteristic features in conduct and construction which strongly evidence both original design and national development.

Angustus William Von Schlegel observes:—

"Among the Indians, the people from whom perhaps all the cultivation of the human race has been derived, plays were known long before they could have experienced any foreign influence."

THE CHARACTER OF THE HINDU DRAMA

Sanskrit plays are full of lyrical passages describing scenes or persons presented to view, or containing reflections suggested by the incidents that occur. They usually consist of four-line stanzas. The prose of the dialogue in the plays is often very commonplace, serving only as an introduction to the lofty sentiment of the poetry that follows.

The Sanskrit drama is a mixed composition in which joy is mingled with sorrow, in which the jester usually plays a prominent part, while the hero and heroine are often in the depths of despair. But it never has a sad ending. The emotions of terror, grief, or pity, with which the audience are inspired, are therefore always tranquillised by the happy termination of the story. Nor may any deeply tragic incident take place in the course of the play; for death is never allowed to be represented on the stage. Indeed, nothing considered indecorous, whether of a serious or comic character, is allowed to be enacted in the sight or hearing of the spectators, such as the utterance of a curse, degradation, banishment, national calamity, biting, scratching, kissing, eating, or sleeping.

Love, according to Hindu notions, is the subject of most of their dramas. The hero, who is generally a king, and already the husband of a wife or wives, is suddenly smitten with the charms of a lovely woman, sometimes a nymph, or, as in the case of Sakuntala, the daughter of a nymph by a mortal father. The heroine is required to be equally impressible, and the first tender glance from the hero's eye reaches her heart. With true feminine delicacy, however, she locks the secret of her passion in her own breast, and by her coyness and reserve keeps her lover for a long period in the agonies of suspense. The hero, being reduced to a proper state of desperation, is harassed by other difficulties. Either the celestial nature of the nymph is in the way of their union, or he doubts the legality of the match, or he fears his own unworthiness, or he is hampered by the angry jealousy of a previous wife. In short, doubts, obstacles and delays make great havoc of both hero and heroine. They give way to melancholy, indulge in amorous rhapsodies, and become very emaciated. So far the story is decidedly dull, and its pathos, notwithstanding the occasional grandeur and beauty of imagery, often verges on the ridiculous. But, by way of relief, an element of life is generally introduced in the character of the Vidushaka, or Jester, who is the constant companion of the hero; and in the young maidens, who are confidential friends of the heroine, and soon become possessed of her secret. By a curious regulation, the jester is always a Brahman, and, therefore, of a caste superior to the king himself; yet his business is to excite mirth by being ridiculous in person, age, and attire. He is represented as grey-haired, hump-backed, lame and hideously ugly. In fact, he is a species of buffoon, who is allowed full liberty of speech, being himself a universal butt. His attempts at wit, which are rarely very successful, and his allusions to the pleasures of the table, of which he is a confessed votary, are absurdly contrasted with the sententious solemnity of the despairing hero, crossed in the prosecution of his love-suit. His clumsy interference with the intrigues of his friend, only serves to augment his difficulties, and occasions many an awkward dilemma. On the other hand, the shrewdness of the heroine's confidantes never seem to fail them under the most trying circumstances; while their sly jokes and innuendos, their love of fun, their girlish sympathy with the progress of the love-affair, their warm affection for their friend, heighten the interest of the plot, and contribute not a little to vary its monotony.

Indeed, if a calamitous conclusion be necessary to constitute a tragedy, the Hindu dramas are never tragedies. They are mixed compositions, in which joy and sorrow, happiness and misery, are woven in a mingled web,—tragi-comic representations, in which good and evil, right and wrong, truth and falsehood, are allowed to mingle in confusion during the first acts of the drama. But, in the last act, harmony is always restored, order succeeds to disorder, tranquillity to agitation; and the mind of the spectator, no longer perplexed by the apparent ascendancy of evil, is soothed, and purified, and made to acquiesce in the moral lesson deducible from the plot.

In comparison with the Greek and the modern drama, Nature occupies a much more important place in Sanskrit plays. The characters are surrounded by Nature, with which they are in constant communion. The mango and other trees, creepers, lotuses, and pale-red trumpet-flowers, gazelles, flamingoes, bright-hued parrots, and Indian cuckoos, in the midst of which they move, are often addressed by them and form an essential part of their lives. Hence the influence of Nature on the minds of lovers is much dwelt on. Prominent everywhere in classical Sanskrit poetry, these elements of Nature luxuriate most of all in the drama.

The dramas of Bhavabhuti except Malati-Madhava, and the whole herd of the later dramatic authors, relate to the heroic traditions of the Ramayana and the Mahabharata, or else to the history of Krishna; and the later the pieces are, the more do they resemble the so-called 'mysteries' of the middle ages. The comedies, which, together with a few other pieces, move in the sphere of civil life, form, of course, an exception to this. A peculiar class of dramas are the philosophical ones, in which abstractions and systems appear as the *dramatis personæ*. One very special peculiarity of the Hindu drama is that women, and persons of inferior rank, station, or caste are introduced as speaking the *Prakrit* or vulgarised Sanskrit, while the language of the higher and more educated classes is the classical Sanskrit of the present type.

THE CONSTRUCTION OF THE SANSKRIT DRAMA

According to the code of criticism laid down in works on Sanskrit drama, it should deal principally either with the sentiment of love, or the heroic sentiment; the other sentiments should have a subsidiary position. There should be four or five principal characters, and the number of acts should vary from five to ten.

There are several species of the drama,—ten principal, and eighteen minor. Of these none has a tragic end.

Every drama opens with a prologue or, to speak more correctly, an introduction designed to prepare the way for the entrance of the dramatis personæ. The prologue commences with a prayer or benediction (*Nandi*) invoking the national deity in favour of the audience.

Then generally follows a dialogue between the stage-manager and one or two of the actors, which refers to the play and its author, mentions past events and present circumstances elucidating the plot, and invariably ends by adroitly introducing one of the dramatic personages, and the real performance begins.

The play thus opened, is carried forward in scenes and acts; each scene being marked by the entrance of one character and the exit of another. The stage is never left vacant till the end of an act, nor does any change of locality take place till then. The commencement of a new act is often marked, by an introductory monologue or dialogue spoken by one or more of the *dramatis personæ*, and is called *Viskambhaka* or *Praveshaka*, which alludes to events supposed to have occurred in the interval, and the audience are prepared for national plenty and prosperity, addressed by one of the principal personages of the drama, to the favourite deity. The development of the plot is brought about through five divisions called the five *sandhis*. A *sandhi* is a combination of incidents whereby the object is attained.

THE MANNER OF PERFORMANCE

There were no special theatres in the Hindu Middle Ages, and plays seem to have been performed in the concert-room (*Sangita-Cala*) of royal palaces. A curtain, divided in the middle, was a necessary part of the stage arrangement; it did not, however, separate the audience from the stage, as in the Roman theatre, but formed the back-ground of the stage. Behind the curtain was the tiring-room (*nepathya*), whence the actors came on the stage. When they were intended to enter hurriedly, they were directed to do so "with a toss of the curtain." The stage scenery and decorations were of a very simple order, much being left to the imagination of the spectator, as in the Shakespearian drama. Weapons, seats, thrones, and chariots appeared on the stage; but it is highly improbable that the latter were drawn by the living animals supposed to be attached to them. There may have been some kind of ærial contrivance to represent celestial chariots.

KALIDASA

Kalidasa is the author of Sakuntala, Vikramorvasi and Malavikagnimitra. He has been designated the Indian Shakespeare. He is reputed to have been one of the nine ornaments (or "gems") of the Court of Vikramaditya, king of Ujayin, whose Era, called *Samvat*, begins in 56 B.C. Stories extant about him describe him to be the veriest fool. He rose to be a great poet through the favour of the Goddess of Learning. Those stories embody the public opinion that except through Divine Grace or the Inspiration of the Muse a man cannot rise to such eminence by learning and culture alone. His native place is Kashmir or its neighbourhood. He had no doubt suffered from the pangs of poverty and neglect and travelled a great deal. He professed the *Saiva* form of worship.

His chief poems are the Raghuvansam, the Kumarasambhavam, the Meghadutam and the Ritusanharam. It is believed that he wrote a treatise on Astronomy and one on Sanskrit Prosody. His genius was of a versatile[Pg 135] nature. He was a poet, a dramatist and an astronomer. His works bespeak the superior order of his scholarship—his acquaintance with the important systems of philosophy, the Upanishads and the Puranas;—his close observation of society and its intricate problems;—his delicate appreciation of the most refined feelings, his familiarity with the conflicting sentiments and emotions of the human heart,—and his keen perception of and deep sympathy with the beauties of Nature. His imagination was of a very high order and of a constructive nature. His power of depicting all shades of character,—high and low,—from the king to the common fisherman, is astonishing. His similes are so very apt that they touch directly the heart and at once enlist the sympathy of the reader. He is called the poet of the sentiment of Love as this sentiment was his *forte*. His diction is chaste and free from extravagance and is marked by that felicity of expression, spontaneity and melody which have earned for him the epithet—"the favoured child of the Muse."

SAKUNTALA

Of all Sanskrit dramas, Sakuntala has acquired the greatest celebrity. It is not in India alone that it is known and admired. Its excellence and beauty are acknowledged by learned men in every country of the civilised world. It was the publication of a translation of this play by Sir William Jones, which Max Muller thinks "may fairly be considered as the starting point of Sanskrit Philology." "The first appearance of this beautiful specimen of dramatic art," he continues, "created, at the time, a sensation throughout Europe, and the most rapturous praise was bestowed upon it by men of high authority in matters of taste."

THE MORAL OF THE PLAY

The recovery of the ring, like its loss, was a matter of pure accident and points to the moral that the joys and sorrows of human beings depend in most cases upon circumstances which lie beyond their control.

MALAVIKAGNIMITRA

The play was not written at a time when Buddhism was

despised, and had already been driven out of India, but when it was still regarded with favour, and was looked up to with reverence.

VIKRAMORVASI

The root of all the stories of Pururavas and Urvasi were short proverbial expressions, of which ancient dialects are so fond. Thus—'Urvasi loves Pururavas,' meant 'the sun rises'; 'Urvasi sees Pururavas naked,' meant 'the dawn is gone'; 'Urvasi finds Pururavas again,' meant 'the sun is setting.'

The same ideas pervade the mythological language of Greece.

BHAVABHUTI

The name of Bhavabhuti stands high in Sanskrit literature. It is perhaps the highest in eloquence of expression and sublimity of imagination. Throughout the whole range of Sanskrit literature— from the simple lessons of Hitopadesha to the most elaborate polish of Naishadha—from the terse vigour of Sankaracharjya to the studied majesty of Magha—from the harmonious grace of Kalidasa to the ornate picturesqueness of Kadambari, there is probably no writer who can come up to Bhavabhuti in his wonderful command of Sanskrit language and surprising fluency and elevation of diction.

The introductions to the Viracharita and the Malati-Madhava tell us that he belonged to Padmapura in Vidarva (Berar) and was the grandson of Gopal Bhatta and son of Nilkantha and Jatukarni. He was descended from a family of Brahmans surnamed Udambaras.

His wonderful memory and vast erudition soon procured for him the title of Srikantha or Minerva-throated. He soon removed to the court of Ujjayini, where before the celebrated Mahakala all his plays were acted.

He wrote the Viracharita, the Uttarramacharita and the Malati-Madhava.

According to Rajatarangini, Bhavabhuti was patronized by Yasovarma, king of Kanoja. This Yasovarma was subdued by Lalitaditya, king of Kasmira, who acquired by his conquests a paramount supremacy over a large part of India.

VIRA CHARITA

The play throws some light on the condition of women. The princesses of Videha publicly go to the hermitage of Vishvamitra. Sita comes out with her attendants to dissuade Rama from meeting Jamadagnya and makes a public entry with him on his return to Ayodhya. The old queens come out to meet their children. Yet it must not be supposed that Hindu women enjoyed the same freedom of intercourse as their European sisters. As now, there used to be separate apartments for women. As now, they were not admitted to an equality with men. The princesses of Videha do not carry on conversation with the princes of Ajodhya. Sita does not come out to pay her respects to the seniors, but her salute is announced from within. There is now more seclusion of Hindu women as the result of the influence of past Mahammedan rule. The influence of British rule is now promoting the cause of female liberty.

UTTARRAMACHARITA

The mutual sorrows of Rama and Sita in their state of separation are pleasingly and tenderly expressed. The meeting of the father and his sons may be compared advantageously with similar scenes with which the fictions of Europe, both poetical and dramatic, abound. The true spirit of chivalry pervades the encounter of the two young princes with their father. Some brilliant thoughts occur, the justice and beauty of which are not surpassed in any literature. The comparison of Chandraketu to a lion's cub turning to brave the thunderbolt is one of these; and another is the illustration of the effects of education upon minds possessed or destitute of natural gifts.

MALATI-MADHAVA

The marriage dress of high-born females described in the sixth act is well worthy of our observation. It consisted of a corset of white silk and a fine red upper garment, besides the usual lower dress, ornaments, and a chaplet of flowers. It has received several modifications since the days of Bhavabhuti.

The sacrifice of good-looking girls, alluded to in the fifth act, was common in his time and other authors allude to it. The seventh story of Dasakumar Charita is just like it, when a prince rescues a princess from a similar Sanyasi and afterwards marries her.

The story of "Malati and Madhava" is one of pure invention. The manners described are purely Hindu without any foreign admixture. The appearance of women of rank in public, and their exemption from any personal restraint in their own habitations, are very incompatible with the presence of Muhammedan rulers. The licensed existence of Buddha ascetics, their access to the great, and their employment as teachers of science, are other peculiarities characteristic of an early date; whilst the worship of Siva in his terrific forms, and the prevalance of the practices of the Yoga, are indications of a similar tendency.

MUDRA RAKSHASA

It must be acknowledged, that the political code from which the stratagems of Chanakya emanate, exhibits a morality not a whit superior to that of the Italian school; but a remarkable, and in some respects a redeeming principle, is the inviolable and devoted fidelity which appears as the uniform characteristic of servants, emissaries, and friends.

The play is wholly of a political character, and represents a series of Machiavellian stratagems, influencing public events of considerable importance.

The Mudrarakshasa is, in sundry respects, a very unique work in Sanskrit literature. Its plot is not a pure invention, but on the other hand, it is not derived from the usual storehouse of legends on which Sanskrit authors have generally drawn for their materials. It has no female among its prominent *dramatis personæ*, and the business of the play, accordingly, is diplomacy and politics, to the entire exclusion of love. There is, in truth, but one female character, with one little child, introduced into the play, and these are Chandanadasa's wife and son, who come in at the beginning of the last act. But even their appearance introduces no passages suggestive of tenderness or the purely domestic virtues, but only of sacrifice—a stern sense of duty.

In the minor characters we see the principle of faithfulness to one's lord, adhered to through good report and evil report. In the more prominent ones, the same principle still prevails, and the course of conduct to which it leads is certainly quite Machiavellian. And all this is brought out in a plot put together with singular skill.

In the seventh act we have a remarkable stanza, in which the conduct of Chandanadasa, in sacrificing his life for his friend

Rakshasa, is stated to have transcended the nobility even of the Buddhas. It seems that this allusion to Buddhism belongs to a period long prior to the decay and ultimate disappearance of Buddhism from India. In the time of Hionen-Tsang—*i.e.* between 629-645 A.D.—it was, however, still far from being decayed, though it appears to have fallen very far below the point at which it stood in Fa-Hian's time, to have been equal in power with Brahminism only where it was supported by powerful kings, and to have been generally accepted as the prevailing religion of the country only in Kashmir and the Upper Punjab, in Magadha and in Guzerat. In this condition of things, it was still quite possible, that one not himself a Buddhist—and Visakhadatta plainly was not one—should refer to Buddhism in the complimentary terms we find in the passage under discussion.

The late Mr. Justice Telang observes:—"The policy of Chanakya is not remarkable for high morality. From the most ordinary deception and personation, up to forgery and murder, every device is resorted to that could be of service in the achievement of the end which Chanakya had determined for himself. There is no lack of highly objectionable and immoral proceedings. It must be admitted that this indicates a very low state of public morality, and the formal works on politics which exist certainly do not disclose anything better. With reference to the criticisms which have been based on these facts, however, there are one or two circumstances to be taken into account. In the first place, although this is no excuse, it may be said to be an extenuation, that the questionable proceedings referred to are all taken in furtherance of what is, in itself, a very proper end. Chanakya's ambition is to make his protegé, Chandragupta firm upon his throne, and to bring back Rakshasa to the service of the king who properly represented those old masters of his to whom Rakshasa's loyalty still remained quite firm. If the end could ever be regarded as justifying the means, it might be so regarded in this case. And, secondly, it must not be forgotten, that the games of diplomacy and politics have always been games of more or less doubtful morality. When we hear of one great politician of modern days declaring another to be a great statesman, because, as I believe he expressed it, the latter lied so cleverly, we cannot say that the world has risen to any very perceptibly higher moral plane in the times of Metternich and Napoleon, than in those of Chanakya and Rakshasa. Nor are suppressions of important passages in despatches for the purposes of publication, or wars undertaken on unjustifiable and really selfish pretexts, calculated to convince one, that even in Europe in the nineteenth century, the transaction of political affairs has been purged of the taint of immorality, however different, and I may even add, comparatively innocent, may be the outward manifestations of that taint."

VISAKHADATTA

Visakhadatta or Visakhadeva is the author of Mudrarakshasa. We learn from the Introduction to the drama that Visakhadatta was the son of Prithu and grandson of Vatesvaradatta—a Samanta or subordinate chief Professor Wilson was inclined to think that Maharaja Prithu might be the Chouhan Prince Prithu Rai of Ajmir; but he himself pointed out that the Chouhan Prince was never called Maharaja; and that the name Nateswara Datta would present a serious difficulty in the way of identifying the poet's father with the Chouhan Prince Prithu Rai of Ajmir. It will also appear that the author of the drama lived in a century which is prior to the age of Prithu Rai of Ajmir by centuries. He was in all probability a native of Northern India. The grandson of a tributary chief and the son of a Maharaja he was well-skilled in statecraft and made a special study of stratagems and crooked policies; in consequence of which the bent of his mind was mainly directed to business and did not indulge in sentiments. The effect of it is manifest in his poetry which is business-like and vigorous, but lacks in sweetness, beauty and the tender emotions.

YAYATI CHARITA

The author may possibly be Pratapa Rudra Deva, sovereign of Telingana in the beginning of the fourteenth century.

DUTANGADA

It is said to have been written for the yatra of Kumar Pala Deva, by order of Tribhuvana Pala Deva, by the poet Subhata.

DHANANJAYA VIJAYA

It is the composition of Kanchana Acharya, the son of Narayana, a celebrated teacher of the *yoga*, of the race of Kapi Muni.

MRIGANKALEKHA

The drama was composed by Viswanath, the son of Trimala Deva, originally from the banks of the Godaveri, but residing at Benares, where it was represented at the *yatra*, or festival, of Visweswara, the form under which Siva is particularly worshipped in that city.

KAUTUKA SERVASWA

This is a Prahasana or Farce, and is especially a satire upon princes who addict themselves to idleness and sensuality, and fail to patronize the Brahmans.

It was composed by a Pandit named Gopinath for representation at the autumnal festival of the *Durga Puja*.

CHITRA YAJNA

This heterogeneous composition is the work of a Pandit of Nadiya, Vaidyanath Vachespati Bhattacharya, and was composed for the festival of Govinda, by desire of Iswar Chandra, the Raja of Nadiya.

HASYARNAVA

This comic play is a severe but grossly indelicate satire upon the profligacy of Brahmans assuming the character of religious mendicants. It satirizes also the encouragement given to vice by princes, the inefficacy of ministers, and the ignorance of physicians and astrologers.

It is the work of a Pandit named Jagaddisa, and was represented at the vernal festival; but where, or when, it is not known.

RATNAVALI

Although the personages are derived from Hindu history, they are wholly of mortal mould, and unconnected with any mystical or mythological legend; and the incidents are not only the pure inventions of the dramatist, but they are of an entirely domestic nature.

It is stated in the prelude to be the composition of the sovereign, Sri Harsa Deva. A king of this name, and a great patron of learned men, reigned over Kashmir; he was the reputed author of several works, being, however, only the patron, the compositions bearing his name being written by Dhavaka and other authors.

RAJA SEKHAR

Raja Sekhar is the author of Prachanda Pandava, Biddhasal-vanjika, and Karpura Manjari.

MURARI

Murari composed Anargha Raghava.

VENISANHARA

The author is Bhatta Narayana surnamed Mrigaraja or Simha, "the lion." He is one of the five Brahmins who, with five Kayesthas, came from Kanouj and settled in Bengal at the invitation of Adisura, the then king of Bengal.

PROBODHA CHANDRODAYA

This play was composed by Krishnamisra. It is an allegorical play, the *dramatis personæ* of which consist entirely of abstract ideas, divided into two conflicting hosts.

HANUMANANATAKA

The play is a dramatized version of the story of Rama interspersed with numerous purely descriptive poetic passages. It consists of fourteen acts and on account of its great length is also called the Mahanataka, or the great drama.

Tradition relates that it was composed by Hanuman, the monkey general, and inscribed on rocks; but, Valmiki, the author of the Ramayana, being afraid lest it might throw his own poem into the shade, Hanuman allowed him to cast his verses into the sea. Thence fragments were ultimately picked up by a merchant, and brought to King Bhoja, who directed the poet Damodara Misra to put them together, and fill up the lacunæ; whence the present composition originated. Whatever particle of truth there may be in this story, the "Great Drama" seems certainly to be the production of different hands.

VASAVADATTA

Vasavadatta of Subandhu is a short romance, of which the story is this.

Kandarpaketu, a young and valiant prince, son of Chintamani king of Kusumapura, saw in a dream a beautiful maiden of whom he became desperately enamoured. Impressed with the belief, that a person, such as was seen by him in his dream, had a real existence, he resolves to travel in search of her, and departs, attended only by his confidant Makaranda. While reposing under a tree in a forest at the foot of the Vindhya mountains, where they halted, Makaranda overhears two birds conversing, and from their discourse he learns that the princess Vasavadatta, having rejected all the suitors who had been assembled by the king her father for her to make choice of a husband, had seen Kandarpaketu in a dream, in which she had even dreamt his name. Her confidante, Tamalika, sent by her in search of the prince, had arrived at the same forest, and was discovered there by Makaranda. She delivers to the prince a letter from the princess, and conducts him to king's palace. He obtains from the princess the avowal of her love; and her confidante, Kalavati, reveals to the prince the violence of her passion.

The lovers depart together: but, passing through the forest, he loses her, in the night. After long and unsuccessful search, in the course of which he reaches the shore of the sea, the prince, grown desperate through grief, resolves on death. But at the moment when he was about to cast himself into the sea, he hears a voice from heaven, which promises to him the recovery of his mistress, and indicates the means. After some time, Kandarpaketu finds a marble statue, the precise resemblance of Vasavadatta. It proves to be she; and she quits her marble form and regains animation. She recounts the circumstances under which she was transformed into stone.

Having thus fortunately recovered his beloved princess, the prince proceeds to his city, where they pass many years in uninterrupted happiness.

www.ingramcontent.com/pod-product-compliance
Lightning Source LLC
LaVergne TN
LVHW011407080426
835511LV00005B/421